1/96

DANGEROUS FLORA

The Encyclopedia of Danger

DANGEROUS ENVIRONMENTS

DANGEROUS FLORA

DANGEROUS INSECTS

DANGEROUS MAMMALS

DANGEROUS NATURAL PHENOMENA

DANGEROUS PLANTS AND MUSHROOMS

DANGEROUS PROFESSIONS

DANGEROUS REPTILIAN CREATURES

DANGEROUS SPORTS

DANGEROUS WATER CREATURES

CHELSEA HOUSE PUBLISHERS

The Encyclopedia of Danger

DANGEROUS FLORA

Missy Allen
Michel Peissel

CHELSEA HOUSE PUBLISHERS
New York   Philadelphia

The Encyclopedia of Danger includes general information on treatment and prevention of injuries and illnesses. The publisher advises the reader to seek the advice of medical professionals and not to use these volumes as a first aid manual.

On the cover   Watercolor painting of a Castor Bean Plant by Michel Peissel.

Chelsea House Publishers

Editor-in-Chief   Richard S. Papale
Managing Editor   Karyn Gullen Browne
Copy Chief   Philip Koslow
Picture Editor   Adrian G. Allen
Manufacturing Director   Gerald Levine
Systems Manager   Lindsey Ottman

The Encyclopedia of Danger
Editor   Karyn Gullen Browne

Staff for DANGEROUS FLORA
Text Editor   Marian Taylor
Production Editor   Marie Claire Cebrián–Ume
Editorial Assistant   Laura Petermann
Designer   Diana Blume

3 5 7 9 8 6 4 2

Library of Congress Cataloging–in–Publication Data

Peissel, Michel, 1937–
Dangerous flora/Michel Peissel, Missy Allen.
p. cm.—(The Encyclopedia of danger)
Includes bibliographical references and index.
Summary: Examines twenty–three dangerous plants found in the world, from the agave to the snow–on–the–mountain.
ISBN 0–7910–1786–9
      0–7910–1939–X (pbk.)
1. Poisonous plants—Juvenile literature. 2. Dangerous plants—Juvenile litera-ture. [1. Poisonous plants. 2. Dangerous plants. 3. Plants.] I. Allen, Missy. II. Title. III. Series: Peissel, Michel, 1937– Encyclopedia of danger.
                                                                    91–45218
QK100.A1P44 1992   CIP
581.6′9—dc20   AC

CONTENTS

THE ENCYCLOPEDIA OF DANGER

"Mother Nature" is not always motherly; often, she behaves more like a wicked aunt than a nurturing parent. She can be unpredictable and mischievous—she can also be downright dangerous.

The word *danger* comes from the Latin *dominium*—"the right of ownership"—and Mother Nature guards her domain jealously indeed, using an ingenious array of weapons to punish trespassers. These weapons have been honed to a fatal perfection during millions of years of evolution, and they can be insidious or overwhelming, subtle or brutal. There are insects that spray toxic chemicals and insects that go on the march in armies a million strong; there are snakes that spit venom and snakes that smother the life from their victims; there are fish that inflict electric shocks and fish that can strip a victim to the bones; there are even trees that exude poisonous gases and flowers that give off a sweet—and murderous—perfume.

Many citizens of the modern, urban, or suburban world have lost touch with Mother Nature. This loss of contact is dangerous in itself; to ignore her is to invite her wrath. Every year, hundreds of children unknowingly provoke her anger by eating poisonous berries or sucking deadly leaves or roots; others foolishly cuddle toxic toads or step on venomous sea creatures. Naive travelers expose themselves to a host of unsuspected natural dangers, but you do not have to fly to a faraway country to encounter one of Mother Nature's sentinels; many of them can be found in your own apartment or backyard.

The various dangers featured in these pages range from the domestic to the exotic. They can be found throughout the world, from the deserts to the polar regions, from lakes and rivers to the depths of the oceans, from subterranean passages to high mountaintops, from rain forests to backyards, from barns to bathrooms. Which of these dangers is the most dangerous? We have prepared a short list of 10 of the most formidable weapons in Mother Nature's arsenal:

Grizzly bear.   Undoubtedly one of the most ferocious creatures on the planet, the grizzly needs little provocation to attack, maul, and maybe even eat a person. (There is something intrinsically more terrifying about an animal that will not only kill you but eat you—and not necessarily in that order—as well.) Incredibly strong, a grizzly can behead a moose with one swipe of its paw. Imagine what it could do to *you*.

Cape buffalo.   Considered by many big-game hunters to be the most evil-tempered animal in all of Africa, Cape buffalo bulls have been known to toss a gored body—perhaps the body of an unsuccessful big-game hunter—around from one pair of horns to another.

Weever fish.   The weever fish can inflict a sting so agonizing that victims stung on the finger have been known to cut off the finger in a desperate attempt to relieve the pain.

Estuarine crocodile.   This vile human-eater kills and devours an estimated 2,000 people annually.

Great white shark.   The infamous great white is a true sea monster. Survivors of great white shark attacks—and survivors are rare—usually face major surgery, for the great white's massive jaws inflict catastrophic wounds.

Army ants.   Called the "Genghis Khans of the insect world" by one entomologist, army ants can pick an elephant clean in a few days and routinely cause the evacuation of entire villages in Africa and South America.

Blue-ringed octopus.   This tentacled sea creature is often guilty of overkill; it frequently injects into the wound of a single human victim enough venom to kill 10 people.

Black widow spider.   The female black widow, prowler of crawl spaces and outhouses, produces a venom that is 15 times as potent as rattlesnake poison.

Lorchel mushroom.   Never make a soup from these mushrooms—simply inhaling the fumes would kill you.

Scorpion.   Beware the sting of this nasty little arachnid, for in Mexico it kills 10 people for every 1 killed by poisonous snakes.

DANGEROUS FLORA

Among the duties assigned to the Federal Drug Administration (FDA) is the recording of poisonings in the United States. For many years, those who most often suffered from accidental poisoning were children; the substance that claimed the most victims was aspirin. Then, in the early 1970s, drug manufacturers began to seal their products with tops—known as childproof caps—that small children found difficult or impossible to open. The result: a sharp drop in cases of aspirin poisoning.

Between 1971 and 1974, Americans became increasingly interested in the raising of both indoor and garden plants. At the same time, more and more people took to the outdoors—camping, backpacking, making nature expeditions. By 1974, this "green explosion" had placed a new culprit at the top of the FDA's child-poisoning list: Mother Nature. In 1990, the American Association of Poison Control Centers reported approximately 63,000 U.S. cases of plant poisoning, more than three-quarters of them involving children under the age of six. Some of nature's most beautiful greenery now presents a very real health hazard in the United States.

In bygone days, Americans lived much closer to nature than most of us do today. Because of their familiarity with the plants around them, our forebears could make safe use of them—as food, as medicine, even as poisons for rats and other unwanted creatures. Accordingly, cases of poisoning were highly unusual (unless they were deliberate, but murder is not our book's subject!). Exceptions occurred, of course, as when immigrants encountered and misused plants previously unknown to them. Other problems could arise when new vegetation was introduced into an area where people were unfamiliar with its potential toxicity.

The *akee* plant, which is discussed in this volume, is a good example of such non-native vegetation and the damage it can cause.

Few Americans can identify more than a handful of flowers, plants, or trees. Fewer still can point out poisonous species, with the possible exception of poison ivy. As long as most citizens lived in the cities, limiting their plant exposure to an occasional bouquet of cut flowers and the annual Christmas tree, ignorance about the natural world posed little threat. But the countermigration out of U.S. cities, combined with the surge of interest in camping and the dramatic increase in the cultivation of houseplants and gardens has put many people at risk.

Plant Toxins

Plant toxins, like the toxins found in many animals, influence their bearer's survival. When a potential enemy—animal or human—realizes that a plant may cause illness or a skin irritation, that enemy will tend to avoid the plant, prolonging the plant's life and the success of its species.

In many of the plant species discussed in this volume, toxins, or poisons, accumulate only in certain parts, such as the leaves, the roots, or the berries. Any poisonous plant's degree of toxicity may vary from one geographic area to another. Toxins from these plants cause injury in three different ways: they can create allergic reactions—usually respiratory—with their windblown pollen; they can produce dermatitis, or skin irritation, by direct or indirect contact; and they can produce internal poisoning, its severity varying according to a victim's size and age, the amount he or she has ingested, and his or her sensitivity to poisons and general state of health.

Prevention

Particularly susceptible to poisoning by the plants discussed in this volume are children, who are often tempted to eat colorful but dangerous seeds and berries or to chew on fleshy or hollow stems that contain powerful toxins. The strongest defense against plant poisoning is knowledge: becoming familiar with the appearance, name, growing habits, and geographic distribution of dangerous plants.

Also important in the prevention of poisoning are the following simple rules:

1. Keep all poisonous plants out of the reach of small children and pets.

2. Do not attempt to make herbal remedies.

3. Do not put plants or plant parts in your mouth, and do not use them as playthings or as skewers for meat or marshmallows.

4. Keep syrup of ipecac, which induces vomiting, on hand as a first aid measure in case of poisoning.

KEY

HABITAT

FOREST

SEA

WOOD/TRASH

TOWNS

SHORE

GRASS/FIELDS

MOUNTAINS

SWAMP/MARSH

GARDEN

FRESH WATER

JUNGLE

BUILDING

DESERT

CITIES

KEY

HOW IT GETS PEOPLE

INGESTION

TOUCH

STING

BITE

SPIT

SPRAY

MAUL

CLIMATIC ZONE

TEMPERATE

TROPICAL

ARCTIC

MORTALITY

ONE

TWO

THREE

FOUR

13

AGAVE

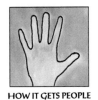

HOW IT GETS PEOPLE

Family: Amaryllidaceae

HOW IT GETS PEOPLE

HABITAT

HABITAT

CLIMATIC ZONE

CLIMATIC ZONE

RATING

Plants of the genus *Agave* are, like the cactus, a common feature of North America's southwestern desert landscape. Among the agave's approximately 150 species is the century plant (*Agave americana*), which blooms only once in its 10-to-15-year life span, then dies. Other species of the agave furnish a variety of products, including fiber, soap, and mescal, a colorless but potent alcoholic beverage popular in Mexico.

The agave is also prized as an ornamental plant: a tall, robust specimen can add welcome green to an otherwise monochromatic southwestern garden. No serious desert gardener, on the other hand, will allow his or her oasis to be marred by a dead agave—a shriveled, brown, and generally depressing sight. Yet to remove such an eyesore requires care. The plant's sharp "teeth" and spines are easy to see and avoid, but many people fail to heed the dangers in the plant's sap.

Towering and beautiful, the agave has delighted nature lovers for centuries, but it has harmful properties as well as pleasing ones. Those who underestimate them can be in for an unpleasant awakening. One homeowner, for example, chopped down an unwanted agave and found his back covered with a painful, burning rash. He had cut the plant with a machete (a large, heavy knife used for harvesting sugar cane and clearing underbrush); after every blow, he had swung the tool over his bare shoulder to prepare for the next stroke. Each time he did, intensely irritating sap had run from the machete's blade onto his back, causing the rash.

In another case, a gardener wanted to trim the lower leaves of the large agave in his yard. To steer clear of the leaves' prickly edges, he did the job with his power mower—which spattered the sap in all directions, including that of the gardener. After developing a severe rash, he took a shower to alleviate the irritation, but that only made matters worse. The blisters remained troublesome for an entire week.

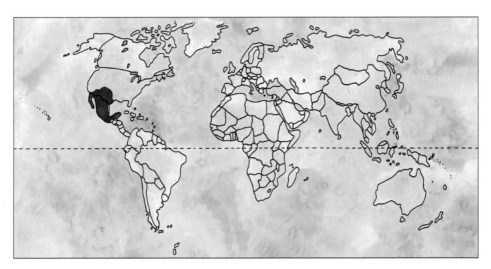

Another agave species, the sisal plant (*Agave sisalana*), supplies tough fibers that are woven into rope or shredded into stuffing for mattresses and cushions. In this form, too, agave can present problems, as in the case of a Florida woman who experienced serious difficulties because of the plant. For more than a year, the woman slept badly and awoke feeling dizzy and depressed. She finally discovered the source of her distress: her mattress, which was filled with a mixture of cotton and sisal fibers. Sisal has been demonstrated to create severe allergic reactions in some individuals; for the Florida woman, it had triggered chronic respiratory problems.

Name/Description

Part of the amaryllis family, *Agave* is a large genus of plants that flourish in Mexico, the southwestern United States, and Central and South America. A perennial (evergreen), the *Agave* genus comprises about 150 species. Nearly trunkless, an agave is formed of a rosette of 10 to 30 tough, flat leaves (six to eight feet long) edged with spines and tipped with a sharp point. Usually after 10 to 15 years of growth, during which the plant stores the nourishment it will need for flowering, the agave flowers once, producing a three–inch–long greenish yellow flower atop an erect, thick stalk up to 30 feet tall. After flowering, the agave withers, but from the base of the stem, it often produces suckers, which become new plants. The agave also produces tiny bulbs (bulbils), which drop to the ground, take root, and grow.

Pharmacology

The thick, reddish roots of some species of agave have been used in folk medicine mixtures, but so far their medicinal value has not been scientifically demonstrated.

Toxicology

The sap of the agave plant contains saponin and oxalic acid. *Agave lecheguilla* also contains an as yet unidentified substance that produces

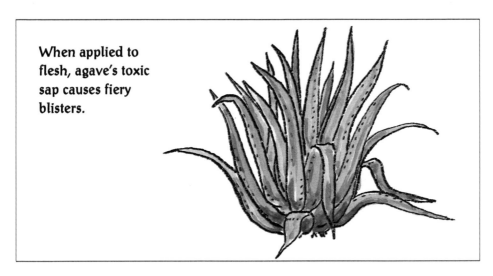

When applied to flesh, agave's toxic sap causes fiery blisters.

photosensitive reactions. (Photosensitivity is an exaggerated sensitivity to light.) Dried, the fibers can produce an allergic reaction.

Symptoms

The saponin in the sap of the agave produces dermatitis (inflammation of the skin) in varying degrees of severity; it can also trigger photosensitization. Contact with the sap triggers an instant sensation of burning in the skin, followed by a red rash and itching welts and blisters. If the sap is quickly and completely removed, these symptoms will disappear in a few days, and the blisters will dry up. The inhalation of dust from dried sisal may, depending on the sensitivity of the individual involved, produce such problems as sneezing, watering of the eyes, shortness of breath, and dizziness.

Treatment

Thoroughly clean the affected area with an antiseptic. To relieve itching, apply a soothing substance, such as calamine lotion. If the reaction is severe, corticosteroids may be given orally or topically. Allergic respiratory symptoms can be relieved with antihistamines.

AKEE

HOW IT GETS PEOPLE

Species: Blighia sapida

HABITAT

CLIMATIC ZONE

RATING

Akee is the common name of both a tree of the botanical family Sapindaceae (soapberry) and its edible fruit. A native of West Africa, akee (called *isin* in its native land, *arbre fricassé* in Haiti, and *seso vegetal* in Cuba and Puerto Rico) bears the botanical name *Blighia sapida*. The species (the only member of the genus *Blighia*) is named after Captain William Bligh, the British naval commander who first described it. It was introduced to the New World in 1788, probably by a British sea captain who brought it to Jamaica as a potential food source for the island's numerous black African slaves.

Nicknamed "Breadfruit Bligh" by fellow British naval officers, William Bligh became aware of the nutritious breadfruit during his 1772 voyage with celebrated explorer James Cook. Intending to load his ship, HMS *Bounty*, with young breadfruit trees and carry them to the West Indies, Bligh sailed to the South Pacific in 1787. He treated his crew with extreme harshness, and in April 1789 they rebelled, setting Bligh and 18 loyal sailors adrift in a small open boat.

Miraculously, Bligh managed to sail the craft across 3,600 miles of ocean, arriving safely in a Dutch harbor one month later. Two years after that, Bligh returned to the South Pacific and this time successfully loaded a batch of breadfruit trees and brought them to the West Indies. The climate of Jamaica and other Caribbean islands proved hospitable to breadfruit, but by then the islanders had developed a special fondness for the fruit that bears the name of Captain Bligh.

Akee soon became one of Jamaica's most popular foods. When cooked, usually by parboiling and then frying, the fleshy arils of the akee are said to have a pleasant texture and a nutty flavor, particularly tasty when served with bacon or fish. The favorite akee dish is *seso vegetal*, or "vegetable brain," so called because the cooked arils resemble a human brain. Delicious as it may be, however, akee presents serious—and sometimes fatal—problems. Between the years 1886 and 1950, for example, approximately 5,000 Jamaicans reportedly died as a result of eating akee.

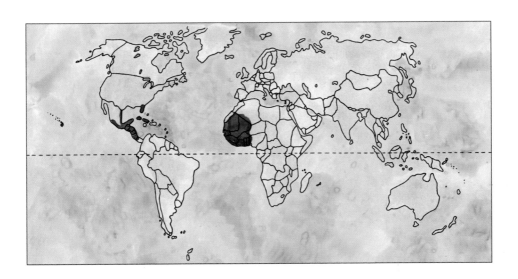

Name/Description

Reaching from 30 to 40 feet in height at maturity, the akee bears small, fragrant, greenish white flowers, which are followed by clusters of three–inch–long, yellow, orange, or red fruit pods. Characteristically, each capsule–shaped, leathery–skinned pod encloses three sections; each section contains a single shiny black seed, which is embedded in an *aril*, a thick, white, fleshy stalk saturated in oil. When the fruit ripens, the sections "yawn," as Jamaicans put it—that is, they split from end to end, revealing the seeds.

Pharmacology

Akee has no known medicinal value.

Toxicology

The rind of the akee fruit contains saponin, a toxic substance some-times used to poison fish. Akee seeds, which contain hypoglycin A (a cyclopropyl amino acid), are poisonous at all times. Before the fruit has opened naturally, the aril is also poisonous; in its unripe state it, too, contains hypoglycin A. Because of the aril's high concentration of oil, it spoils quickly after ripening, becoming toxic as well.

Symptoms

Ingestion of the skin, black seeds, or aril (unripe or overripe) of the akee can produce sudden and violent vomiting, followed by convulsions, coma, and death. Also toxic is the water in which unripe arils have been boiled; many victims have added this "pot liquor," with poisonous results, to codfish stew or vegetable dishes. "Vomiting sickness" occurs in Jamaica in periodic waves, mostly in the winter months, when unripe arils are more often available on the market. Undernourished children appear particularly susceptible to akee poisoning. Despite the cases of

Ingestion of unripe akee fruit or seed can result in a bout of the highly unpleasant "vomiting sickness."

akee poisoning, Jamaicans continue to eat their beloved vegetable brain. The government has, however, banned the further canning of akee fruit for export.

Treatment

Supply fluids and glucose to replace those lost through vomiting. In the case of undernourished children, a doctor should administer intravenous vitamin supplements along with glucose.

Prevention

- Do not eat vegetable brain or other dishes made from akee. When visiting Jamaica, make sure that no one has added akee pot liquor to soups, stews, or other foods you plan to eat.

BELLYACHE-BUSH

HOW IT GETS PEOPLE

Species: Jatropha gossipiifolia

HOW IT GETS PEOPLE

HABITAT

CLIMATIC ZONE

RATING

The bellyache–bush has a split personality: widely respected as a medicine, it is also feared as a poison. Its seeds, according to many residents of South and Central America, not only produce stomach distress but cure it as well. In Mexico, where the bush is called the *mala mujer*, or "evil woman," it is often blamed for the deaths of those—usually children—who eat its seeds. Filipinos poison fish with its leaves, catching the dead fish as they float to the water's surface.

In its native Brazil, the bellyache–bush gives light: Brazilians use oil from the plant's seeds to fuel their lamps. Common in the tropics, the bush is becoming more and more popular in the southeastern United States, where it is often misleadingly marketed as the "African coffee tree," a garden ornamental. Clearly a plant of many applications, the bellyache–bush is still best known for its medical uses—which, according to some believers, are little short of fantastic.

Name/Description

The bellyache-bush is a three-to-six-foot-tall annual shrub with a short main stem. Its few spreading branches, which are hairy toward the tips, contain a translucent, yellowish, sticky, toxic sap. The plant's leaves, each with three to four lobes, are more or less hairy on the underside; its small flowers, dark red with yellow centers, resemble coral. The fruit of the bellyache-bush is an oval capsule, three-sided, one-half inch long, and green until it dries and turns brown. When the fruit is ripe, each of its three sections opens, releasing one black or mottled seed about one-quarter of an inch long.

Pharmacology

Residents of the West Indies have long used the leaves of the bellyache-bush in a decoction (extract produced by boiling) to relieve stomach-aches. Venezuelans and Colombians claim that the plant's upper leaves produce vomiting and that the lower leaves have a laxative effect.

People in the Netherlands Antilles count on the bellyache-bush for first aid; applied to cuts and scratches, they say, sap from the bush stops bleeding and relieves pain and itching. The bellyache-bush is even said to work on cancer. Many people on the Caribbean island of Aruba believe that a decoction of peeled and mashed stems from the plant cures throat cancer, and large numbers of Costa Ricans swear by the plant's root as a cancer cure.

Someday, some of these claims may prove more reasonable than they sound today. Researchers at the University of Virginia have discovered some evidence that jatrophine, a growth-inhibiting principle derived from the root of the bellyache-bush, shows activity against human throat cancer cells.

Toxicology

The ingestion of a single seed from the bellyache-bush can cause severe poisoning. The seeds contain three toxic elements: jatrophine (curcin); cathartic oils, which cause bowel evacuation; and a plant lectin (toxalbumin), which inhibits protein synthesis in the cells of the intestinal wall, creating a potentially fatal condition. The latex of the bellayache-bush contains saponin.

Symptoms

Unlike other plants containing toxic lectins, the bellyache-bush produces immediate symptoms: a burning sensation in the throat, bloating, nausea, dizziness, deafness, severe gastroenteritis (inflammation of the lining membrane of the stomach and intestines), vomiting, and diarrhea. Severe cases may also produce drowsiness, dysuria (painful or difficult urination), leg cramps, and violent diarrhea before death. Contact with sap from the bush can cause dermatitis.

If ingested, a single seed from the bellyache-bush can be fatal.

Treatment

Dehydration from vomiting should be corrected with fluid replacement; because of severe throat irritation, these fluids may have to be given by intravenous injection.

Dermatitis can be treated by the application of a soothing lotion, such as calamine.

CASTOR BEAN

HOW IT GETS PEOPLE

Species: Ricinus communis

RATING

HABITAT

HABITAT

CLIMATIC ZONE

CLIMATIC ZONE

The castor bean plant (sometimes called Palma Christi) is a native of Africa but is now widely raised both in tropical zones, where it is a perennial, and in temperate zones, where it is an annual. It is extensively cultivated both as an ornamental plant and as a commercial source of oil, which is extracted from its seeds.

Until the middle of this century, castor oil—a thick, nauseating liquid extracted from castor beans—was considered the "sovereign remedy" for constipation and the promotion of regular bowel habits. The countless children forced to swallow this unpleasant substance surely looked upon it as a type of poison. Unlike the deadly seeds from which it is made, however, castor oil is quite safe and has been used for thousands of years in one way or another.

The ancient Egyptians, who gave castor oil a name that roughly translates as "nauseous to the taste," kept it outside their bodies. Herodotus, the Greek historian who lived and wrote some 500 years before the Christian Era, observed that "the Egyptians who live in the marshes use for the anointing of their bodies an oil made from the castor berry." The Egyptians also used castor oil as lighting fuel; it was, said Herodotus, "as well suited as olive oil for lamps, only that it [gave] out an unpleasant odor." The first-century Roman scholar and natural scientist Pliny the Elder recognized castor oil as far more than a harsh laxative:

> It is good also for diseases of the joints, for all indurations [numbness], for the uterus, the ears and burns . . . and likewise for the itch. It improves the complexion, and through its fertilizing power it promotes the growth of hair. The seed from which it is made no living creature will touch.

Unfortunately, Pliny was quite mistaken in what he said about "living creatures"—especially in the case of small, human ones who are attracted by the shiny castor bean seeds. These harmless-looking objects contain ricin, one of the most toxic substances the world has ever known. Ingestion of these seeds is, in fact, one of the major causes of poisoning among children in the southern United States. Said to have quite a pleasant taste, castor bean seeds are readily available in gardens across the South. Both children and adults sometimes make necklaces

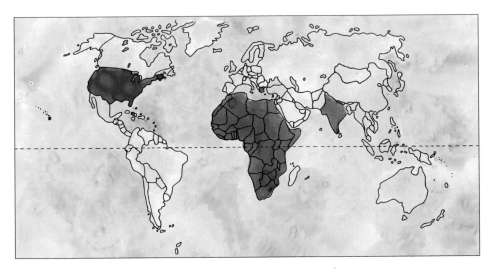

from the beans, which is not a safe practice; the hole through which the string passes can also allow seepage of toxic material from the inside onto the skin.

The ferocity of the castor bean's poison, ricin, was dramatically demonstrated in a London assassination some years ago. Georgi Markov, a 49-year-old Bulgarian exile and journalist, was waiting for a bus when he felt a sudden jab in the back of his right thigh. A nearby man apologized, then jumped into a cab and vanished. Three days later, Markov was dead. Doctors suspected poison but could find no traces of it nor any way it could have been administered. Then, during the autopsy, they discovered a pinhead-sized, hollow metal ball embedded in the back of Markov's leg. The sphere could contain only a microscopic amount of poison, leading the experts to conclude that nothing could have killed Markov except the deadly ricin.

As well as being used as poison, medicine, lamp oil, and body lotion, castor oil is also employed as an industrial lubricant.

Name/Description

A member of the Euphorbiaceae family, the castor bean plant grows to a height of 15 feet in temperate areas, and in the tropics to a height of 40 feet. Its impressive foliage—star-shaped green leaves highlighted with bronze and measuring as much as three feet across—makes it an attractive and popular addition to many gardens. The plant's oval, green or red fruit is covered with fleshy spines and contains three small, smooth, black or mottled grayish brown seeds.

Pharmacology

For thousands of years castor oil has been used as a laxative.

Toxicology

The seeds of the castor bean plant contain ricin, a plant lectin that inhibits synthesis in the intestinal wall. Ingestion of the beans is often fatal.

In the southern United States, ingestion of castor bean seeds is a leading cause of childhood death.

Symptoms

Symptoms, which develop several hours after ingestion, consist of a burning feeling in the mouth, throat, and stomach, along with vomiting, diarrhea, and abdominal cramps. From the second to the tenth day there may be bleeding and low blood pressure, possibly leading to shock. Complications may develop, leading to convulsions and death. Nonfatal poisoning may result in permanent damage to the intestines, liver, and kidneys.

Treatment

If the victim is conscious and alert, induce vomiting. A doctor may wish to administer *gastric lavage*, a procedure in which the poison is literally washed out of the stomach. Contents of the victim's stomach are siphoned out via a tube in the throat; after that, a cleaning solution is piped through the tube to cleanse the stomach completely. The doctor will probably also keep the patient's urine alkaline with 5–15 grams of sodium bicarbonate daily. The doctor may later give an antacid to reduce local irritation caused by vomiting.

COCA

HOW IT GETS PEOPLE

Species: Erythroxylon coca

HABITAT

CLIMATIC ZONE

RATING

For centuries, South American Indians, particularly those of the Andes Mountains in Peru, have chewed the leaves of the coca plant, which provided them with increased energy, decreased pain, and the ability to ignore hunger.

Line drawings on pottery discovered in northwestern South America indicate that the chewing of coca leaves was a widespread practice before the beginning of the Inca Empire, possibly as early as 3,000 years before the Christian Era. Coca leaves have been found in ancient pre-Inca graves; archaeological evidence shows that in the 10th century, the Incas of Peru, who called coca the "divine plant," employed it as an offering to the sun and used it to produce smoke during ceremonies of sacrifice.

When the Spanish conquistadores arrived in South America in the 16th century, they were astonished by the natives' ability to "walk forever" and by the extraordinary feats of endurance achieved by message–bearing long–distance runners. Believing that the use of coca made the Indians less likely to become Christian converts, the Spanish at first attempted to curb the practice. Then, realizing that if they allowed the Indians to use coca, they could extract almost superhuman labor from them in the gold and silver mines, the Spanish began to encourage consumption of the plant.

Even today, the miners of Cerro de Pasco in Peru chew cocaine, spitting the masticated leaves against the walls of the mine in the belief they will soften the veins of ore. Cocaine addiction is still a grave problem in South America, where there are believed to be at least 20 million addicts, most of them in Peru. Many Peruvian Indians still carry a *chupsa* (leather pouch), to hold coca leaves and pulverized unslaked lime, which facilitates the drug's absorption through the membranes of the mouth. Three or four times a day, labor is suspended for *chachar* (mastication of coca).

In 1886, John S. Pemberton, a druggist in Atlanta, Georgia, mixed up his first batch of a new soft drink, which he called Coca-Cola. The name came from the beverage's two main ingredients: dried coca leaves and cola, the extract of the bitter, caffeine-containing seed of the kola tree. Pemberton produced 25 gallons of Coca-Cola syrup, then sold its formula (for $2,300) to Atlanta businessman Asa Griggs Candler.

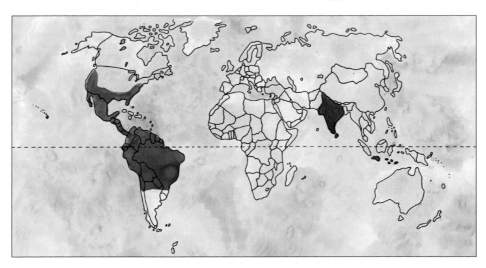

Advertising the stimulating drink as the "intellectual soda-fountain beverage" and a surefire remedy for "Tired Brain," Candler turned it into a major industry and made "Coke" almost as symbolic of the United States as the Stars and Stripes. Today's standard Coca-Cola retains its caffeine, but its cocaine has been replaced with completely decocainized coca leaves, used for flavor. The modern drink is thus quite lacking in the narcotic effect produced by chewing coca leaves.

Tragically, now almost as universal as Coca-Cola is cocaine addiction, which leaves its victims—if they do not die from an overdose—with psychological disturbances, malnutrition, deterioration of the nervous system, and digestive problems.

Name/Description

The coca plant, *Erythroxylon coca*, of the family Erthroxylaceae, is an evergreen shrub native to South America but also widely raised in Southeast Asia and Australia. Reaching heights of 12 feet, it has bright green, bristly, oval leaves two to three inches long, and small, yellowish white flowers that grow in little clusters on short stalks. The blossoms are succeeded by red berries. Coca is cultivated mainly in the mountain valleys of Peru, Colombia, and Bolivia.

Pharmacology

The alkaloid cocaine, extracted from coca leaves, is used as a topical anesthetic to the nose, mouth, or throat, allowing some types of surgery or examinations to take place without pain.

Toxicology

Coca leaves contain the white crystalline alkaloid cocaine, which is a narcotic. Massive quantities of cocaine ingested by any route of administration can result in central nervous system damage, elevated blood pressure, cardiac failure, and death. Cocaine smugglers sometimes try to escape detection by swallowing a condom or a balloon filled with the drug; several have died when the packet broke, resulting in the absorption of excessive amounts of cocaine.

Some South American Indian tribes chew on coca leaves to increase their strength and endurance.

Symptoms

A cocaine overdose, known as cocaine hydrochloride poisoning, can produce overstimulation of the central nervous system, followed by depression, nausea, dizziness, tingling of hands and feet, fever, anxiety, rapid respiration, numbness of the tongue, cyanosis (bluish discoloration of the skin due to insufficient oxygen in the blood), delirium, and coma or convulsions with wide dilation of the pupils. Cocaine alters the normal electrical activity of the brain; an overdose may result in seizures, repeated convulsions, and death.

Treatment

For acute poisoning, a physician should administer diazepam intravenously, induce vomiting, or administer gastric lavage; otherwise treat symptomatically. Activated charcoal may be administered orally to absorb the poison. Artificial respiration and oxygen may be needed. If a patient survives three hours after an acute attack, the prognosis is generally good.

CURARE

HOW IT GETS PEOPLE

HABITAT

CLIMATIC ZONE

RATING

An alkaloid extracted from several South American plants, curare was and is an arrow poison used by the Indian hunters of the Amazon and Orinoco river basins. Its original name, *woorari*, is an Indian word for "poison." Although the substance has been the subject of intensive interest since the time of Christopher Columbus, chemists were not able to unlock its secrets until the mid-20th century.

In 1555, Italian writer-explorer Pietro d'Anglera described a battle in which Guianan Indians (residents of the region bordering present-day Brazil and Venezuela) killed some 30 Spanish soldiers with arrows dipped in curare. "The poison is of such force," wrote d'Anglera, "that albeit the wounds were not great, yet they died thereof immediately." Sir Walter Raleigh, the great English navigator and historian, described the poisonous "ourari" and its usage in his 1596 book, *The Discoverie of the Empire of Guiana.*

The Indians, noted Raleigh, applied the curare to the tips of arrows or darts, which they fired from blowguns, 10-foot-long bamboo poles lined with hollow reeds. The needle-sharp ends of the wooden darts were dipped in curare, and their blunt ends wrapped in cotton to make them fit more snugly in the blowgun. Deadly accurate in the hands of a skilled hunter, a blowgun could send its missile as far as 300 feet. Each tribe had its own secret recipe for curare.

In 1828, Charles Waterton, an adventurous Briton who had spent several years exploring Brazil's Amazon valleys, published a travel book,

Wanderings in South America. In it, the author discussed the curare used by the Macusi Indians of British Guiana, fearsome hunters whose darts and arrows were said to kill a man or beast instantly and painlessly.

Deciding that curare might be of use in treating such convulsive diseases as rabies, Waterton sealed a quantity of the poison in wax balls and carried it back to England. There, he experimented on hens, dogs, a three-toed sloth, and a 900-pound ox. Working with several trained scientists, Waterton soon discovered that curare acted on its victim's muscles, relaxing them to the point of paralysis. Death, he realized, came to curare's victims when the muscles used in breathing became paralyzed.

In 1935, scientists established that the active ingredient of the various forms of curare was tubocurarine, the alkaloid product of several South American trees. Eight years later, chemists succeeded in producing pure alkaloid d–tubocurarine from *Chondondendron tomentosum*, a plant that also provided the neuromuscular blocking agent tubocurarine chloride (trademarked as Intocostrin), a substance administered to relax skeletal muscles in surgery.

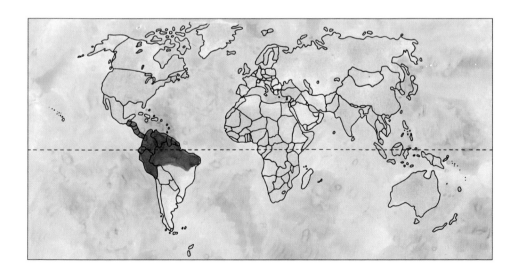

Curare continues to be extensively used in medicine—and as a poison. In the mid-1960s, 13 patients at a New Jersey hospital run by a South American doctor, Mario E. Jascalevich, died mysteriously. When the bodies of the 13 were exhumed a decade later, autopsies discovered traces of curare. Jascalevich, who had been known for his experiments with curare, was accused of murder. Although he was acquitted after a long trial, he lost his medical license and returned to South America.

Name/Description

Curare is a generic term applied to various plant extracts employed as arrow poisons by the Indians of northern South America and now used medicinally. The most important constituent of curare is an alkaloid from the moonseed vine, *Chondondendron tomentosum*, which is usually mixed with extract from the poison nut *Strychnos toxifera*. A woody vine that winds itself snakelike from tree to tree, the chondondendron is sometimes called "bush rope." The vines have rough, dark gray bark and dark green oval leaves. The fruit of the poison nut is the size of an apple and is round, smooth, and bluish green with seeds embedded in a bitter-tasting pulp. Many other species of *Chondondendron* and *Strychnos* are used as secondary ingredients of curare, their role to assist absorption of the poison from the arrow.

Pharmacology

Even before doctors fully understood how curare works, they used it as a muscle relaxant in treating diseases such as tetanus ("lockjaw"), whose symptoms include a tightening of the muscles. Today, curare's major clinical use is in surgery; in carefully graded doses it relaxes the patient's muscles, making it easier for the surgeon to incise the skin without excessive anesthesia. Curare has also been used to treat such orthopedic conditions as dislocations and muscular spasms.

Toxicology

The most important curare poison is the alkaloid d-tubocurarine, which is extracted from *C. tomentosum*. The curare poisons act on the precise

Curare is sometimes used as a surgical tool: it relaxes muscles and therefore facilitates incision.

point where nerves and muscles join. Normally, the nerves that connect with muscles produce acetylcholine, a chemical that passes from the nerve to the muscle and makes it contract. Curare blocks acetylcholine, making it impossible for the muscles to contract. Instead they relax com–pletely. Other principles are toxiferines, curacurines, and other alkaloids.

Symptoms

Injection of curare will produce haziness of vision; relaxation of facial muscles; inability to raise the head; and loss of muscle control in arms, legs, and lungs. Curare usually kills by causing respiratory failure. Rubbed on the skin or ingested in small amounts, curare is relatively harmless—unless there is a cut on the skin or inside the mouth, in which case poisoning will occur.

Treatment

There is no known antidote. Indians believed, correctly, that curare victims would live if the poison was sucked out of their wounds; they also knew that if the rescuer's mouth was cut or contained a sore, he or she would be poisoned.

ELEPHANT'S EAR

HOW IT GETS PEOPLE

Species: Colocasia gigantea

HOW IT GETS PEOPLE

HABITAT

HABITAT

HABITAT

CLIMATIC ZONE

CLIMATIC ZONE

RATING

U.S. poison control centers periodically release "Top 20" lists—inventories of the substances that draw the most worried inquiries. Usually ranking near the top of these lists is the elephant's ear, a huge tropical plant that, for some reason, strongly tempts children's appetites. With leaves that can grow as long as four feet, the elephant's ear is often bigger than the children who bite on it.

The plant is widespread, low growing, and tender, perhaps explaining the appeal it exerts on youngsters. Harder to explain, however, is the fact that large numbers of children take not just an exploratory nibble from the elephant's ear but whole mouthfuls: when chewed, all parts of the plant produce an immediate and painful burning sensation in the lips, tongue, and throat.

As well as seriously stinging the mouth, the elephant's ear can produce other problems. One plant expert, Julia F. Morton, has written about a couple who brought her the leaf and stem of an elephant's ear and asked for her advice. Their two-year-old son, said the couple, had picked a similar leaf and started chewing on it before they could stop him. He had started crying, then lapsed into silence, apparently unable to talk. What should they do?

Morton told the worried parents that their son's problem would undoubtedly disappear soon. The highly irritating juice of the elephant's ear leaf, she said, had probably caused the boy's throat to swell temporarily, accounting for his silence. She suggested cool, soothing drinks and advised the parents to keep their child away from such "pretty leaves" in the future. As she had predicted, he recovered quickly; the plant's painful and sometimes frightening effects rarely last long.

Surprisingly, elephant's ear is not only an irritant; it is also a food. When cooked, its long, tubular, yellow rhizome (underground stem) is

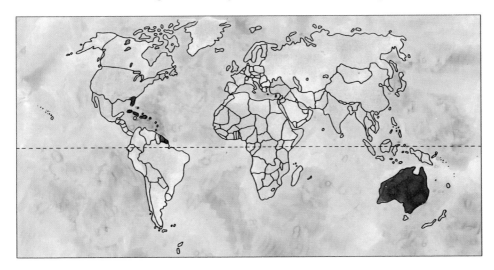

harmless and, some say, delicious. Widely served as a starchy vegetable in Cuba, Puerto Rico, and other tropical locales, the boiled rhizome—known as *malanga*, *yautía*, and *tanier*—is also increasingly popular in the southeastern United States, current home to numerous Caribbean immigrants.

Name/Description

The name *elephant's ear* is applied to several species in the Araceae family. The *Alocasia* is a popular house plant, as is the *Caladium*, sometimes known as angel wings, Heart of Jesus, or lágrimas de María (Mary's tears) as well as elephant's ear. The *Xanthosoma sagittifolium* can be safely eaten when cooked; the *Xanthosoma violaceum*, or purple-stemmed taro, is another widely used garden plant. The *C. palustris*, also known as water arum and water dragon, grows in swampy areas throughout the United States and Canada. The smallest member of the family, *Calla palustris* measures only about 12 inches in height; it bears thick clusters of red berries in the fall. Elephant's ear plants vary in appearance: some have soft, showy white leaves veined in green; others are green veined in red; still others produce stiff green leaves blotched with white. They range in height from 1 to 15 feet.

Pharmacology

No species of the Araceae family has yet proved medically useful.

Toxicology

Containing calcium oxalate raphides (a strong skin irritant composed of needlelike, stinging crystals), all members of the Araceae family can cause injury to humans.

Symptoms

Biting on any part of any of these plants when they are raw will immediately produce a severe sensation of burning in the mouth and

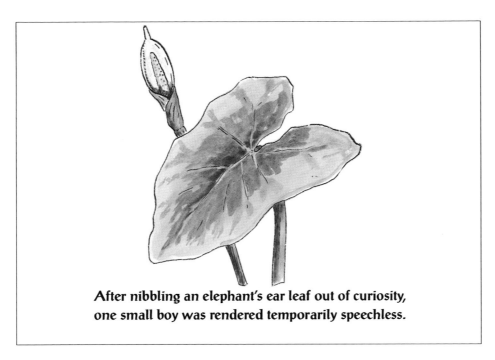

After nibbling an elephant's ear leaf out of curiosity, one small boy was rendered temporarily speechless.

throat. The burning feeling is followed by swelling of the lips and tongue and, if the sap is ingested, by stomach pain. The sap can cause eye irritation on contact. It may also result in a rash around the mouth or dermatitis (inflamed areas on the skin) wherever it touches. Hoarseness or difficulty in speaking may also develop temporarily.

Treatment

Give milk or ice cream to soothe the mouth and throat; sucking on ice chips may bring relief from intense pain. Closely observe any swelling of the tongue and mouth that could obstruct the upper air passage. Antihistamines may provide relief from severe swelling, and analgesics may be given for pain. For eye irritation, flush the eye with tepid water for 15 minutes. For skin irritation, wash the skin thoroughly with soap and water, then apply a soothing lotion, such as calamine.

BLACK HELLEBORE

HOW IT GETS PEOPLE

Species: Helleborus niger

CLIMATIC ZONE

HABITAT

HABITAT

RATING

Like many other poisonous plants, black hellebore has a long history as a poison, medicine, and "magic powder." Also known as the Christmas rose (it flowers in winter), black hellebore was said, in ancient times, to cure madness and to be effective in treating paralysis, gout, and other ailments. The ancients also reportedly used it as a chemical weapon. Six hundred years before the Christian Era, an Athenian general threw hellebore roots into the drinking supply of a city he was besieging. The enemy soldiers, according to a historian of the time, "drank without stint, and those on the wall, seized with obstinate diarrhea, deserted their posts, and the [Athenians] captured the city."

Although the ancient Greeks called the hellebore's rhizome the "bread of death," they used it for snuff: they dried and powdered the rhizomes, producing a dark brown dust that they inhaled "to quicken their wits." The same powder was once believed to render people invisible. Witches, according to an old French legend, would shower themselves with ground black hellebore roots so that no one could see them flying about on their witchy errands.

Name/Description

Black hellebore, or *Helleborus niger*, is a member of the family Ranunculaceae, among whose approximately 700 species are also such familiar plants as the marsh marigold, the peony, and the buttercup. A perennial, hellebore has a stout rhizome and reaches a maximum height of about two feet. Its leathery, ovate (egg-shaped) leaves, which are slightly toothed at the apex (tip), remain throughout the winter. The showy flowers are two to three inches across, with white or pinkish white petaloid (like a petal) sepals (outer covering of the flower). The fruit is a small capsule containing numerous glossy black seeds.

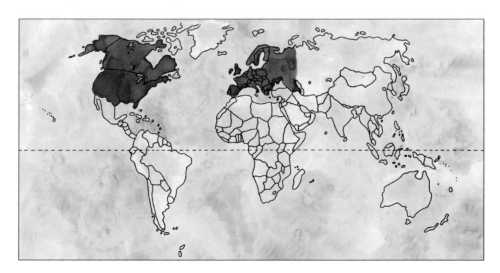

Pharmacology

Although black hellebore plays no part in modern medical practices, it was once used to treat everything from excessive bleeding at childbirth to cerebral hemorrhage (copious bleeding in the brain) to intestinal parasites. Medical history suggests that hellebore sometimes produced good results, but that it more often proved highly dangerous. Until relatively recent times, for example, British doctors employed the rhizome of the hellebore as a vermifuge (a substance that expels worms and other parasites from the intestinal tract) for children. Results of this treatment varied, noted one medical authority: "Where it killed not the patient, it would certainly kill the worms; but the worst of it is, it will sometimes kill both."

Extract of the black hellebore's rhizome has also been used to calm the insane. As late as 1900, British doctors were employing hellebore as a sedative for heart and "nerve" patients, as an antihemorrhagic medication, a purgative, and a uterine stimulant. Hellebore rootbark and seeds were used to treat cancer, tumors, ulcers, warts, and indurations (hardenings), especially of the spleen. Veterinarians, too, made use of hellebore in treating their patients, especially horses.

Toxicology

The entire plant is poisonous. Its toxic principles are hellebrin, helleborin, and helleborein. The plant's aerial parts (leaves, stems, and flowers) contain ranunculin or protoanemonin.

Symptoms

Ingestion produces immediate pain in the mouth and abdomen, followed by nausea, vomiting, cramps, and diarrhea. Other symptoms may be excitement and restlessness, paralysis of the legs, ringing in the ears, vertigo (a sensation of dizziness; an illusion of movement), stupor, thirst, and a feeling of suffocation. There may be some cardiac symptoms.

An old French tale claims that witches use hellebore powder to render themselves invisible.

Treatment

Give syrup of ipecac to induce vomiting and call a physician. He or she will probably administer gastric lavage, then activated charcoal to absorb the poison, as well as spasmolytics for the colic. Phenytoin may be given for rhythm disturbances.

HOLLY (AMERICAN)

HOW IT GETS PEOPLE

Genus: Ilex

CLIMATIC ZONE

HABITAT

HABITAT

HABITAT

RATING

To "deck the halls with boughs of holly," as the old Christmas carol urges, is to observe a custom that early Christians probably adopted from the ancient Romans. In celebration of the annual winter solstice, the Romans staged a festival of Saturn, or *Saturnalia*, each mid–December. During the holiday period, they exchanged green boughs and other symbolic gifts with their friends.

The Christian church tried to abolish such pagan customs, but its official prohibition of the use of boughs (and ivy) had little effect, as evidenced by another ancient Christmas carol:

Christmastide
Comes in like a bride,
With holly and ivy clad.

Holly's decorative use has also been traced to the Druids, ancient Celtic mystics who festooned their huts with evergreens during the winter to welcome sylvan (forest) spirits.

According to a medieval legend, the first holly sprang up in footsteps of Jesus Christ, its thorny leaves and red berries recalling his crown of thorns and the blood he shed on the cross. In many northern European countries, the holly tree is known as "Christ's thorn"; in Britain, it is the "holy tree." According to an old folk belief, the holly's white flowers cause water to freeze. To protect themselves against lightning and witchcraft, ancient Britons planted hollies near their homes—a precaution still taken in parts of rural England.

"Vomitoria" is the holly's least attractive name, but it does suggest one of its properties: when eaten, tempting-looking holly berries cause recurrent bouts of vomiting. Children, the plant's most frequent victims, usually become dehydrated from these bouts, which are accompanied by diarrhea.

Native Americans of the southern United States brewed a strong beverage from holly leaves; known as "black drink," it may have played

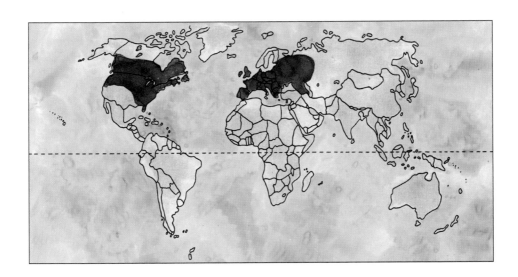

a role in ritual purifications. When real tea was unavailable, early settlers made a mild brew from the leaves, which contain caffeine.

Name/Description

The *Ilex* genus, part of the Aquifoliaceae family, contains three varieties: *Ilex aquifolium* (English holly), *Ilex opaca* (American holly), and *Ilex vomitoria* (yaupon, Carolina tea, or deer berry). All these evergreens can reach heights of 70 feet, but cultivated forms usually average 6 to 15 feet. The holly's thick, glossy leaves are leathery, spiny edged and alternate, each measuring about two inches in length and one and a quarter inches in width. They are edged with stout prickles that grow alternately upward and downward and that remain attached for several years.

In the spring and summer, both male and female holly trees bear multiple small, whitish flowers, but only female trees produce berries, which are brilliant red—or, in the case of the *Ilex vomitoria*, yellow. Holly trees grow very slowly.

Pharmacology

In days past, holly played an important part in folk medicine. A "tea" made with the leaves was believed to promote sweating and hence was given for malaria and other chronic fevers. Healers also used the plant's leaves to reduce common fevers, restore energy, and promote relaxation. Modern experiments suggest that the leaves do have sedative properties, although their effectiveness has not been clinically proven.

Toxicology

Holly berries, which contain saponins, are poisonous. The leaves are nontoxic and, in many species, yield caffeine.

Symptoms

The ingestion of holly berries produces a burning sensation and swelling of the mouth, throat, and tongue. If the swelling is intense, speech can

Ancient legends claim that holly can freeze water, ward off lightning, and protect people from witches' spells.

be impaired. The first symptoms are followed by nausea, multiple episodes of vomiting, and attacks of diarrhea (sometimes bloody).

Treatment

If the victim has not yet vomited but is conscious and alert, give syrup of ipecac to induce vomiting. Milk or water may soothe the irritation of the mouth. Children, who are likely to become dehydrated from the diarrhea, should be given copious fluids.

JUNIPER

HOW IT GETS PEOPLE

Species: Juniperus communis

CLIMATIC ZONE

HABITAT

HABITAT

HABITAT

RATING

People of ancient times linked the juniper tree to the spirit world. When a woman was giving birth, her attendants burned juniper branches, believing that the smoke would prevent the fairies from substituting a child of theirs for the newborn baby. The Minaro, an ancient Aryan people of the western Himalayas, ritually purified themselves by standing over burning juniper, as many Tibetan Buddhists still do.

During the Middle Ages, Europeans believed that juniper smoke would protect them against such dread diseases as the plague and leprosy. Juniper was widely employed as a folk remedy for practically every ailment known, including arteriosclerosis (hardening of the blood–vessel walls), arthritis, bronchitis, cancer, colic, dysentery, gonorrhea, gout, hysteria, rheumatism, snakebite, tuberculosis, tumors, and worms.

By the 17th century, juniper had developed ties to a second spirit world. In the early 1600s, a French prince started using juniper berries (actually, the tree's dried ripe fruit) to flavor a wine that was later distilled to make gin. The name *gin*, in fact, derives from *geneva*, a corruption of *genièvre*, the French word for juniper. Today, juniper berries remain the principal flavoring agent of gin.

Juniper berries are also used in alcoholic bitters, and their extracts and oils are used in most food categories, including candy and desserts, and to flavor game, stuffings, marinades, and stews. Juniper oil is also a fragrance component in soaps, detergents, lotions, and perfumes

Name/Description

Juniper is usually a rather low, evergreen shrub or small tree that grows to heights of four to six feet. Its bark is thin and reddish brown. The sharp, dark, needlelike leaves, one–half to three-quarters of an inch in length, spread at nearly right angles to the twigs. Near the end of the branchlets appear small, yellowish green cones that consist of scales arranged in whorls of three.

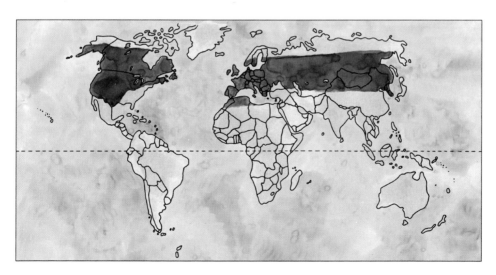

The juniper's small, berrylike fruits start out green, turning blue-black to purple when they mature, two to three seasons after their first appearance. Dried berries become somewhat darker and shrivel slightly; they have a bitter taste. Juniper branches have a disagreeable, penetrating odor, especially when heated. The plant, native both to Europe and North America, grows in dry, rocky soil in fields and woodlands; it especially favors steep hills where lime or limestone is present.

Pharmacology

Modern medicine has little use for juniper, although it is still occasionally used as a urinary antiseptic, particularly in treating cystitis. In bygone days, however, the tree and its berries had many applications: It was used to remove warts and as a remedy for scurvy, worms, and dropsy (an abnormal accumulation of fluid in the cells, now known as edema). It was prescribed for menstrual disorders. Juniper was also long respected as a diuretic (increasing the excretion of urine) and as a carminative (relieving internal gas). Finally, juniper berries were said to induce miscarriages; supposedly this is why, in France, growing juniper was rigorously forbidden for many years.

Toxicology

Juniper-berry oil, which is most abundant just before the fruit ripens, contains a significant amount of monoterpenes, making it somewhat toxic to humans. The oil also contains 4-terpineol, which, when swallowed, can produce kidney irritation and circulatory problems.

Symptoms

Ingestion may cause kidney pain, strong diuresis (urinary discharge), accelerated heartbeat and blood pressure, and abdominal congestion. Major overdoses may produce severe cramps and, occasionally, hal-

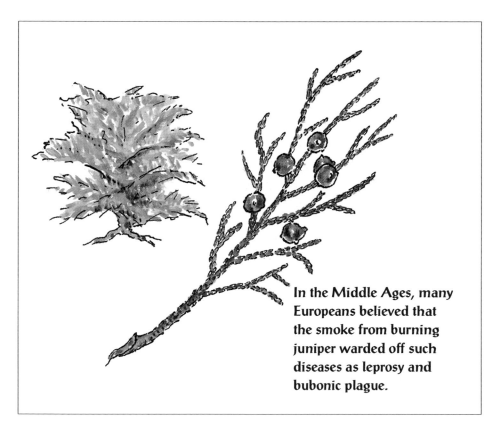

In the Middle Ages, many Europeans believed that the smoke from burning juniper warded off such diseases as leprosy and bubonic plague.

lucinations and death. In rare cases, spontaneous abortions have been attributed to the ingestion of juniper. Juniper's volatile oil can cause skin irritations—burning sensations, redness, blisters, and swelling.

Treatment

A physician may treat a patient who has consumed juniper berries with gastric lavage or, if the poisoning appears less extensive, with simple fluid replacement. Dermatitis may be relieved with a soothing cream, such as calamine.

LOCOWEED

HOW IT GETS PEOPLE

Genus: Astragalus

CLIMATIC ZONE

HABITAT

HABITAT

HABITAT

RATING

The genus *Astragalus*, which contains some 1,600 species, appears all over the world; about 275 of these species are native to western North America. Of this number, four are locoweeds, all of them extremely poisonous, especially to livestock: they are the purple loco (*Astragalus mollissimus*), the blue loco (*A. lentiginosus*), the bigbend loco (*A. earlei*), and the western loco (*A. wootoni*). These plants, which grow in profusion on sandy hillsides and plains west of the Mississippi River, also pose a threat to humans: their pealike pods look edible, especially to children.

Locoweed was named by the Spanish explorers who first encountered it in the 16th century. Its earliest noticeable effect on those who consume it is in the legs; victims move erratically, often staggering and falling. Struck by the plant's strange influence on horses, an Englishman visiting Colorado described it in 1879: "After the animal has eaten the leaves for a little while, the animal seems much exhilarated. It is impossible to handle him. . . . When a horse is locoed, it is easily perceived. Loco is a Spanish word, meaning mad, crack-brained, or foolish, which describes the effects of the weed on horses."

Animals are poisoned by locoweed only after consuming it in large quantities; unfortunately, range animals seem to become addicted to it and often *do* eat it in dangerous amounts. What people find tempting about locoweed is its appearance: it bears a beautiful purple, pink, or white blossom that nods gracefully in the prairie breeze. "The flowers of this dry region," wrote 19th-century naturalist Thomas Meehan, "are famed for their brilliant colors, by which they give a gay and attractive feature to the otherwise dreary scenery of this inland tract. [Locoweed] always has the same showy head of flowers, thrown up above the silvery foliage." The blooms also attract insects, especially bees; the flower nectar produced by one locoweed species in Nevada is so toxic that it has killed whole colonies of honeybees.

Name/Description

Locoweed, also known as milk vetch or poison vetch, is a member of the pea family, Leguminosae. These perennial plants generally grow

in clumps or patches; in the fall, they produce a pod consisting of two longitudinal compartments, each containing one or more kidney-shaped seeds. Locoweed leaves are compound, with many small leaflets on either side of the leaf stem and one at the tip. The plant's pealike, pink-to-purple flowers grow in crowded clusters.

Pharmacology

The milk vetch (*A. glycyphyllos*) was once believed to increase the milk output of goats that nibbled on it; other than that, the locoweed and its cousins have no recorded beneficial attributes—except for their dangerous beauty.

Toxicology

Locoweed leaves, pods, and seeds contain organic nitrogen compounds (glycoside of nitropropionic acid; miserotoxin), consumption of which can lead to acute poisoning in animals and humans. Locoweed plants are dangerous throughout the year, even after they have matured and dried out. Toxicity remains even after storage periods of three years or more.

Symptoms

Signs of locoweed poisoning (also called locoism) include staggering, trembling, and paralysis, as well as sudden, rapid weight loss and loss of sense of direction. Respiratory difficulties (huskiness, coughing, wheezing) may also occur. These symptoms usually appear after an animal has grazed locoweed for two to three weeks.

Treatment

Doctors attending humans who have eaten locoweed ordinarily call for immediate gastric lavage or induced vomiting, or both. For animals, no

The flower nectar produced by one locoweed species in Nevada is so toxic that it has killed whole colonies of honeybees.

effective treatment is known, and recovery seldom occurs. A rancher can protect his or her stock only by keeping animals away from fields where locoweed is present or by eliminating the weed with carefully supervised application of a chemical herbicide.

MANDRAKE

HOW IT GETS PEOPLE

Species: Mandragora officinarum

CLIMATIC ZONE

HABITAT

HABITAT

HABITAT

RATING

The mandrake root, which often resembles a gnarled human figure, has been steeped in superstition for untold centuries. The world over, millions of people once believed that this vegetable's powers—to bring good health, fertility, passion, and death—were boundless.

The ancient Greeks called mandrake *Circeium*, after mythology's Circe, the malevolent sorceress who possessed great knowledge of magical and poisonous plants. Hippocrates, the Greek physician who practiced almost five centuries before the Christian Era, wrote about investigations of mandrake and its effect on humans: a mixture of mandrake and wine, he noted, was thought to relieve depression and anxiety.

Mandrake also figures prominently in military history: Hannibal, the great Carthaginian general, for example, used it to put down a rebellion in the third century B.C. Strewing his campsite with vessels of mandrake wine, he staged a retreat; after the rebels arrived and drank themselves into a stupor, Hannibal returned and slaughtered them. And the Roman emperor Julius Caesar wrote of escaping from enemies by numbing them with mandrake wine.

Ancient medical practitioners offered a number of remedies for mandrake intoxication: bind the victim's head or pour rose oil in one nostril. The most colorful cure directed the healer to seat the patient in a tub, put mint and almond leaves on his head, then annoint him with a hot mixture of olive oil, water, and sharp wine while he drank honeyed, old raisin wine.

The ancient Romans used mandrake as an anesthetic during operations. Its anesthetic virtues were also prized by the women who dedicated themselves to comforting victims of crucifixion, a fairly common Roman method of execution. These women sponged the bodies of those on the cross with morion, an anodyne of mandrake. In Shakespeare's play *Romeo and Juliet*, Juliet receives a sleeping potion made with mandrake and later notes that these "magical" roots have strange properties. They "shreik" when uprooted, so "that living mortals, hearing them, run mad." As well as being somniferous (causing sleep), mandrake was also thought to be an aphrodisiac (something that excited sexual desire). Hoping to promote passion and conception, biblical–era Palestinian women wore amulets containing powdered mandrake root.

In the Middle Ages, mandrake was classified as a "subtle poison," which took about three days to kill its victim. Recipes for the fatal potion called for fermenting the root until it smelled foul, then waiting an additional 60 days. At this point, it was apparently ready to do its worst. This concoction was said to be the one preferred by Lucrezia Borgia, the celebrated 15th–century Italian noblewoman and alleged poisoner.

During the Renaissance, the mandrake's astronomical popularity made it scarce and expensive and created a vast black market where false mandrake roots were sold along with real ones. Mandrake roots often grow in the shape of a human; dealers therefore dug up similar-sized roots, shaped them into humanoid forms, and replanted them to grow further. The roots were often sold to childless women who wished to conceive.

The European passion for mandrake roots developed to the point where 16th–century Germans dressed and bathed their mandrake "dolls" regularly. Said to have special powers, the water that had been used to bathe the mandrakes was sprinkled around the house to protect it and its inhabitants. The ritual of gathering and using mandrake roots finally became so involved and ponderous that by the end of the 17th century, it was losing its appeal. The magical rituals that once obsessed millions of people now exist only as a historical footnote.

Name/Description

Mandrake, a perennial member of the nightshade (Solanaseae) family, is a native of Europe and Asia. The plant has a short stem; waxy, ovate leaves; large flowers varying in color from whitish to purple; golden–colored fruit (in the fall, replacing the flowers); and a thick, often forked root. It reaches a height of about 18 inches.

Pharmacology

In the past, mandrake root was used to treat asthma, arthritis, colic, coughs, hay fever, hepatitis, schizophrenia, and sclerosis. It is still used medicinally in some parts of the world, notably China, where it has traditionally served as an anesthetic.

One legend states
that the mandrake
plant emits a human-
like scream when
pulled from the earth.

Toxicology

Mandrake roots and leaves are highly poisonous, but the berries are edible and even delicious, according to some. The toxic principles are hyoscyamine and scopolamine, which together form mandragorine and other alkaloids. Scopolamine has parasympltolytic properties (restricting the activity of the sweat, salivary, and bronchial glands; inhibition of gastrointestinal motility; relaxation of hollow organs, such as the gall and urinary bladders and the uterus). Scopolamine is also, even in small doses, a motor depressant and at higher doses produces "twilight sleep," a form of light anesthesia.

Symptoms

There will be dryness of the skin, mouth, and throat. The victim will experience difficulty in swallowing, flushing of the face, cyanosis, nausea, vomiting, and slurred speech. There may also be loss of feeling and an insensitivity to pain. In acute poisoning, there will be a noisy delirium (much shouting), and hallucinations before coma and death.

Treatment

If the victim has not already vomited and is awake and alert, give syrup of ipecac to induce vomiting or administer gastric lavage. Give activated charcoal orally to absorb any remaining poison. Otherwise, treat symptomatically.

MESCAL BEAN

HOW IT GETS PEOPLE

Species: Sophora secundiflora

RATING

HABITAT

HABITAT

CLIMATIC ZONE

CLIMATIC ZONE

On hearing of the mescal bean plant, the average person might think of mescal, the Mexican alcoholic beverage, or mescaline, the principal hallucinogenic component in peyote (see Peyote, page 84). Although all three—mescal, mescaline, and mescal beans—can alter one's behavior and perceptions (a hallucinogen induces hallucinations, or perception of unreal sights and sounds), they vary in their long-range effects. Mescal can produce a bad hangover, peyote, a "bad trip." But a mescal bean can kill, even with only slight overdose.

The mescal bean goes by a number of names: *frijolito* (Spanish for "little bean"), Texas mountain laurel, coralillo, pagoda tree, red bean. Until fairly recent times, a number of Indian tribes in New Mexico, Texas, and northern Mexico practiced the Red Bean Dance, a ritual in which participants ingest some form of mescal beans, then see visions. These

Indians, to whom "vision seeking" was a fundamental religious element, sought their visions primarily at times of illness, childbirth, death, and war.

The Red Bean Dance, also known as the Wichita, Deer, or Whistle Dance, utilized the mescal beans both as a hallucinogenic medium and as an oracle—a means through which the Indians could receive communications from a divinity. Some tribes drank a liquid made from the beans; others roasted and crushed the beans, chewing and swallowing the resulting paste. Archaeologists, who have found mescal beans at sites dating back to 1500 B.C., suggest that the beans formed the center of a prehistoric cult.

Deaths from mescal bean overdoses were not uncommon, and sometime in the 18th or 19th century, the Indians began to replace the drug with the peyote cactus, a safer but even more potent hallucinogen. But as Richard Evans Schultes, a Harvard University expert on hallucinogenic plants, has noted, "sacred elements do not often disappear completely from a culture"; today, mescal beans are used as adornments by leaders of the peyote ceremony among the Kiowas, Anadarkos, and other Oklahoma Indians.

In the late 1960s and 1970s, some young people began to use mescal beans recreationally, as they did many other hallucinogenic plants and mushrooms. But these users quickly realized the high risk of fatal overdose and, like the Indians of the Southwest, abandoned the mescal bean.

Name/Description

The mescal bean plant is a member of the bean, or legume, family (Leguminosae). A shrub or tree, it grows up to 35 feet tall with evergreen, compound leaves four to six inches long, each bearing 7 to 13 leathery, smooth–edged, oblong leaflets, and each densely covered with whitish hairs. The plant's violet–scented, purple flowers grow in showy terminal clusters and bloom in spring and summer. Following the flowers are large, jointed cylindrical pods that split open to reveal from one to eight hard, bright red beans or seeds, which average one–half inch in length. Slow growing, this shrub favors sunny, dry limestone hillsides.

Pharmacology

Ancient Indian tribes apparently used mescal beans for medical as well as religious purposes, but they play no part in contemporary medicine.

Toxicology

Mescal beans contain a toxin–pyridine called cytisine, a pharmaceutical cousin of nicotine.

Symptoms

Usually occurring within one hour of ingestion, symptoms of mescal bean poisoning include nausea, vomiting, headache, vertigo (dizziness), excessive salivation and perspiration, and diarrhea. Acute poisonings produce convulsions, delirium, coma, and death through respiratory failure.

**Ingestion of a single mescal bean
can easily kill a child.**

Treatment

With mild intoxications, a physician will probably simply treat the victim's gastroenteritis (inflammation of the lining membrane of the stomach and intestines) and replace lost fluids. Oxygen and respiratory support may be needed occasionally. In some cases, an individual who has ingested mescal beans may experience a disturbing level of excitement; a heavy, inebriated feeling; nausea; and heart palpitations for up to three days, after which he or she may feel irresistibly sleepy for several more days.

MISTLETOE

HOW IT GETS PEOPLE

Species: Phoradendron flavescens

HABITAT

CLIMATIC ZONE

RATING

For centuries, mistletoe has been an essential part of Yuletide decor, inspiring the exchange of countless Christmas kisses. Unfortunately, however, it has also inspired a good number of stomachaches; like those other holiday standards, holly and poinsettia, mistletoe is toxic if eaten.

Mistletoe was the lucky charm that the mythical Trojan hero Aeneas carried with him on his descent into Hades and that brought him safely back. For the people of ancient Europe, mistletoe was sacred, symbolizing the spirit of the fertility god. The cutting of mistletoe from an oak tree was the climax of a rite conducted by the Celtic Druids, in which they severed the mistletoe with a golden blade and caught it in a pure white cloth, which they later burned. Then, underneath the host tree, the priests sacrificed two white bulls to atone for the cutting.

An old Norse myth relates how an enemy killed the young hero, Baldur, with a spear he had fashioned out of mistletoe. At this, the compassionate Freya (the Scandinavian goddess of love and youth) restored Baldur to life and made herself protectress of mistletoe. Its strength was said to depend upon its not touching the earth. (The plant is a parasite, drawing all its nourishment from the tree it climbs on.)

In the Christian tradition, mistletoe was one of dozens of plants identified as the wood of Christ's cross; medieval monks wore bits of mistletoe wood, usually fashioned into crosses, around their necks. The first published report of its fatal effects was probably in Gerarde's 1597 book, *Herball*: "Inwardly taken," he wrote, mistletoe "is mortall, and bringeth most greevous accidents, the toong is inflamed and swolne, the mind is distraughted, the strength of the hart and wits faile."

In spite of this warning and many others since, people have continued to become poisoned with mistletoe; the most frequent victims are children who eat the plant's tempting white berries. Those who regard mistletoe as a Christmas necessity should remember to hang it well out of reach of children and other heedless merrymakers.

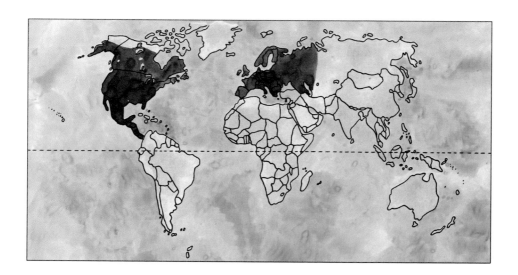

Name/Description

Mistletoe is a parasitic green shrub with thick, leathery, oblong leaves occuring in opposite pairs. It grows on a variety of deciduous trees (those that shed their leaves annually) and has small, yellowish flowers. Reaching heights of one to four feet, the mistletoe has waxy, pinkish white or white globose berries covered with a sticky pulp. "True" mistletoe (*Viscum album*), native to Europe, is toxic but not fatal. About a half–dozen species of the genus *Phoradendron* are found in North and Central America.

Pharmacology

In medieval times, mistletoe was thought to protect against apoplexy, tremors, poisoning, consumption, and other afflictions. It was also recommended for its stimulant property in cardiac treatment. Some Native American tribes on the West Coast believed mistletoe especially valuable as a medicine if it grew on the buckeye tree; they chewed the leaves to relieve toothache. The plant is no longer used in Western medicine.

Toxicology

Mistletoe's leaves and stems are toxic; the berries, if consumed in large numbers, are also poisonous. Mistletoe contains phoratoxin (toxalbumin), which inhibits protein synthesis in the intestinal wall, and an alkaloid.

Symptoms

Ingestion of mistletoe leaves, stems, or berries can create acute stomach and intestinal irritation with vomiting, diarrhea, and slow pulse. In fatal cases, usually triggered by the ingestion of "tea" made with a large quantity of mistletoe leaves, there is failure of the cardiovascular system.

Mistletoe's most common victims are children, who mistake the white berries for edible fruit.

Treatment

Give syrup of ipecac to induce vomiting or administer gastric lavage. Potassium, procainamide, and quinidine sulfate have all been used effectively.

MOUNTAIN LAUREL

HOW IT GETS PEOPLE

Species: Kalmia angustifolia,
K. latifolia, K. microphylla

CLIMATIC ZONE

HABITAT

HABITAT

RATING

One of the most beautiful of America's native plants, mountain laurel was discovered in the 18th century by Peter Kalm, the Swedish botanist who gave his name (*Kalmia*) to its genus. Mountain laurel, a member of the heath family, is often found with its cousins, the azalea and rhododendron, at the edge of a forest. It is not a true laurel but was so named because its smooth, simple, oblong leaves resemble those belonging to plants of the genus *Laurus*.

Another foreign visitor, the English author Frances Trollope, in her 1832 travel book, *Domestic Manners of the Americans*, referred to the mountain laurel she saw in the Allegheny Mountains as "that beautiful mischief." More than mischievous, mountain laurel is downright deadly;

many children have been poisoned by sucking its flowers and making "tea" from its leaves. Even honey from the flowers is poisonous, but fortunately, most people find it too bitter to consume in large amounts.

Animals tend to avoid laurel, but livestock poisonings have been reported during winter months, when little other foliage is available. One of the more widespread mountain laurels, *K. angustifolia*, is, in fact, often called "lambkill" or "calfkill," and ranchers and farmers try to keep their fields clear of it. Zoo directors, too, keep a wary eye on laurel and its cousins: hardy and handsome, they add beauty to zoological parks, but they must be kept out of the animals' reach. Zoo workers have also learned to keep these plants away from visitors; at the zoo in Washington, D.C., animal fanciers accidentally poisoned a valuable monkey and several angora goats by feeding them mountain laurel flowers and leaves.

Mountain laurel was for a long time used as a local remedy for skin diseases and a variety of other ailments, but because of its toxicity and the frequent incidence of overdoses, modern doctors sternly discourage its use.

Name/Description

Mountain laurel is a beautiful evergreen shrub or small tree growing from 6 to 30 feet tall and bearing alternate, ovate leaves two to four inches long. Its numerous, showy, starlike flowers, which appear in a corymb (a cluster of flowers in which the stems are of different lengths, and so arranged along a common axis as to form a flat, broad mass of flowers with a level top), are delicately tinted in shades ranging from pale pink to a dark rose with purple markings. When in full flower, usually in June and July, mountain laurel plants form dense thickets. The stems are crooked, and the bark is rough. The fruit is a dry capsule; the seeds are minute and numerous.

Pharmacology

Powdered leaves were formerly used as a local remedy in some forms of skin diseases and were said to be efficient in treating syphilis, fevers, jaundice, neuralgia, and inflammation. But they were always used with great care because of their toxicity. Homeopathic practitioners some-times recommend mountain laurel for heart problems; taken internally, it is believed to act as a sedative and astringent in active hemorrhages and diarrhea.

Toxicology

Mountain laurel leaves are poisonous, and the toxin in their nectar can poison honey. The plant's poisonous principles are an andromedotoxin (acetylandromedol), arbutin, and tannic acid.

Symptoms

Ingestion of mountain laurel leaves produces a transient burning in the mouth and nose, as well as watering eyes. Several hours after ingestion, a victim will probably experience increased salivation, nausea, vomiting, diarrhea, sweating, and a prickling sensation of the skin. The victim may complain of headache, muscular weakness, and dimness of vision.

At the zoo in Washington, D.C., animal fanciers accidentally poisoned a valuable monkey and several Angora goats by feeding them mountain laurel flowers and leaves.

Bradycardia (slow pulse) is followed by severe hypotension (low blood pressure). In acute poisonings, there may be drowsiness, tingling of the skin, incoordination, convulsions, and increasing limb paralysis until death.

Treatment

Give syrup of ipecac to induce vomiting, or administer gastric lavage. Fluid replacement will be required. Oxygen and respiratory support may be needed. Atropine may be administered for bradycardia. If hypotension is severe, ephedrine should be given. With proper treatment, recovery may be complete in 24 hours.

NUTMEG

HOW IT GETS PEOPLE

Species: Myristica fragrans

HABITAT

CLIMATIC ZONE

RATING

In 1512 Dutch traders returned to Europe from the Moluccas, an archipelago better known as the Spice Islands, with a new spice: nutmeg. Its exotic flavor quickly made nutmeg a highly prized delicacy among Europeans, who especially enjoyed it mixed with wine. A character in *The Knight of the Burning Pestle*, a 1607 play by British dramatist Francis Beaumont, sings:

Nutmegs and Ginger, Cinnamon and Cloves,
And they gave me this jolly red nose.

And the clown in William Shakespeare's 1610 play *The Winter's Tale*, recites a list of ingredients for a shepherd's feast: "I must have . . . Nutmegs, seven; a race or two of ginger, but that I may beg."

Nutmeg also quickly caught on as a medicine; it was especially popular as a carminative. Because of its resemblance to the human brain, nutmeg was thought to be particularly effective for treating mental ailments. Eager Europeans found yet another use for the treasured nutmeg: it could be brewed into a surefire love potion. This notion became so widespread that people began to wrap the spice in silver and suspend it from a chain at the throat.

During the 18th century, merchantmen brought more than 100 tons of nutmeg to Europe every year. Trading in nutmeg and other spices became so lucrative, in fact, that the Dutch, Portuguese, and British went to war over control of the Spice Islands. In 1796 the English took over the island of Banda, the largest producer of nutmeg, and began export-ing nutmeg trees to start new nutmeg plantations in other British colonies.

Nutmeg's reputation continued to spread. By the late 18th century, it was perhaps most valued as protection against infection, especially during plague epidemics. In *The Art of Perfumery*, author G. W. Piesse offered a recipe for "Vinegar of the Four Thieves," a protective substance said to have been used by grave robbers during the Marseilles plague of 1722.

Nutmeg was popular in the United States, too, but it was even more expensive there than in Europe. As a result, sharp traders began to mix counterfeits into sacks of the genuine thing: "Yankee peddlers," wrote Thomas Hamilton in his *Men and Manners in America*, "always have a large assortment of wooden Nutmegs."

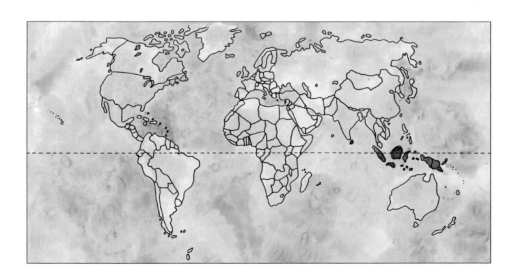

Nutmeg also gained fans because of its power to intoxicate and because of its hallucinogenic properties. Chewing nutmeg seeds, it is said, is similar to smoking marijuana: it can inspire pleasant drowsiness, hallucinations, and a feeling of well-being. People in India who chew betel nut (the seed of a tall palm, mixed with dried betel leaves and lime and used as a stimulant) often add nutmeg, as do some tobacco chewers and snuff dippers.

As is the case with so many other intoxicating plants, overdoses of nutmeg are common and very dangerous. According to a recent medical study, just two whole nutmeg seeds can be fatal. Like any potentially dangerous substance, nutmeg should be kept out of the reach of children.

Name/Description

The nutmeg tree grows to a height of 60 feet. Its branches spread in whorls, an arrangement of stems at about the same point on the trunk. On their tops, the tree's alternate leaves are elliptical, smooth, aromatic, dark green, and glossy; underneath, they are paler. The leaves measure from four to six inches in length. Nine years old before it blooms, the nutmeg tree bears rather inconspicuous yellow flowers that grow in clusters, each appended to its own short stalk spaced along the stem. The fruit, which resembles an apricot, changes from a brilliant scarlet when fresh to yellowish brown when dry. The firm, fleshy aril (seed) is whitish and transversed by red-brown veins; it abounds in oil. A nutmeg tree can keep bearing fruit for 75 years.

Pharmacology

Nutmegs were once used to cure problems of the brain, as a cure for failing eyesight, and as a general tonic. The spice is no longer employed for these purposes, but it is for others: oil of nutmeg is used to conceal the taste of various drugs, as a local stimulant to the gastrointestinal tract, as a remedy for flatulence (gas), and to correct the nausea arising from the ingestion of other drugs.

Though commonly used as a spice, a mild overdose of nutmeg can cause delirium, panic, and hallucinations.

Toxicology

The toxic principle in nutmeg is myristicin; it also contains a volatile oil and a saponin.

Symptoms

A mild overdose caused by ingesting one–third of an ounce of seeds can cause time–space distortions, feelings of unreality, and visual hallucinations accompanied by dizziness, headache, and central nervous system stimulation. In addition, ingestion of more than the above amount may cause acute panic, delirium, convulsions, and even death.

Treatment

As soon as possible after ingestion, give the victim two to four ounces of castor oil. Administer gastric lavage. Later, give a demulcent (a medicine that has a soothing effect on inflamed tissues).

OPIUM POPPY

HOW IT GETS PEOPLE

Species: Papaver somniferum

HABITAT

CLIMATIC ZONE

RATING

The opium poppy, a beautiful flower that thrives in India, parts of Asia and the Middle East, and Mexico, is another of the plants that have both aided and injured humankind. For thousands of years, people have used and abused the opium obtained from the poppy, which can kill pain, stimulate the nervous system, provide euphoria—and lead to mental confusion, physical illness, and death.

Opium and its derivatives—such drugs as laudanum, morphine, and heroin—are extremely addictive. Users, even individuals who start taking these drugs for medical reasons, often begin to crave them, psychologically as well as physically. And the longer a person uses them, the more it takes to obtain the same effect; trying to discontinue drug use is almost always a harrowing experience. As most people of the 1990s know through news reports, observation, or personal experience, drug withdrawal produces nausea, insomnia, mental depression, and hallucinations, among other distressing symptoms.

The opium poppy's powers, both for evil and good, have been known since at least 3000 B.C., when the Sumerians (who lived in what is now Iraq) wrote of the "joy plant." Three millenia later, Arabs, Greeks, and Romans were using opium as an analgesic (pain killer), sedative (tranquilizer), and soporific (sleeping potion). Native to Europe and Asia, the opium poppy has particularly thrived in India and Turkey. Today's principal source for opium and its by-products is the so-called Golden Crescent—Iran, Afghanistan, and Pakistan. The nations of the Golden Triangle—Myanmar (formerly Burma), Thailand, and Laos—also export vast amounts of the drug, as does Mexico.

Wherever they are raised, opium poppies tend to bloom in the late spring, when a vast cloak of gracefully swaying white, lavender, and reddish purple flowers covers acre after acre of land. After two or three days, the poppy's delicate, tissue-thin petals fall. Seed capsules, bulbous and green, remain atop the stalks, steadily swelling, for another week or so. Then workers begin to walk backward among them, performing a ritual at least 2,000 years old.

As they shuffle down the rows, the harvesters make swift, precise cuts in the swollen capsules, slitting the flesh without cutting through to the

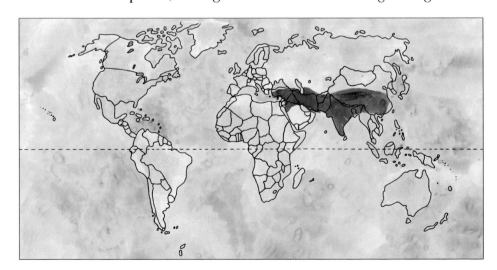

immature seeds inside. Almost immediately a thick whitish fluid oozes from the cuts and starts drying. The next morning the workers return to collect the sun-browned, gummy blobs of opium, which will be processed into heroin. One acre of opium poppies produces about 22 pounds of opium; 10 pounds of opium produces 1 pound of heroin.

Early opium users ate the flowers or made them into liquids and drank them. By about A.D. 600, the Turkish and Islamic cultures of western Asia discovered that opium delivered a stronger effect when it was ignited and smoked. As the centuries passed, more and more people in ever-widening areas took up the practice of opium smoking. Arab merchants brought the drug to India and China; by the 18th century, England's great merchant fleet had started carrying the drug home from the Far East; British doctors and laymen quickly accepted it, both as a medicine and a mood improver, and by the beginning of the 19th century, opium and its by-products were staples in a majority of British homes.

At about this time, Chinese authorities grew worried about the growing number of opium addicts. They tried to prohibit both the cultivation and importation of the opium poppy, but by then, trade in the drug had become a major British profit center, and the British refused to let the Chinese outlaw it. Two conflicts—the Opium Wars of 1839 and 1856—left the British victorious. The opium trade continued.

Meanwhile, Frederick Sertuerner, a Swiss-German chemist, had been trying to isolate the specific narcotic elements of opium. In 1803, he succeeded, deriving a potent crystal alkaloid that he called morphine, after Morpheus, the Greek god of sleep. The mid-19th-century invention of the hypodermic syringe made possible the widespread use of morphine on the battlefield during the American Civil War, which began in 1861.

Morphine eased a great deal of agony, but it was used so freely that it created a huge number of addicts. Morphine addiction became known as the "army disease." Later in the 19th century, a German pharmaceutical company succeeded in chemically modifying morphine to produce an even more powerful opiate: heroin. The drug proved too dangerous

Though opium-based drugs have medical benefits, addiction to the same drugs can be fatal.

for medical use, but it soon found its way to the streets, where it remains, along with other illegal drugs, one of society's most pressing problems.

Name/Description

Opium is from the Greek *opos*, meaning "juice", and refers to the milky-white sap of the poppy's seed capsule. The plant's scientific name, *Papaver somniferum*, means "poppy that brings sleep" and refers to its frequent use as a soporific.

The opium poppy is an erect, herbaceous annual, varying much in the color of its flowers as well as in the shape of the fruit and color of the seeds. The flowers vary from pure white to reddish purple; in the wild they are pale lilac with a purple spot at the base of each petal. The seed capsules are usually hemispherical but depressed at the top, and they have a swollen ring below the point at which the capsule joins the stalk.

The kidney-shaped seeds, minute and very numerous, are attached to lateral projections from the inner walls of the capsule and vary in color from whitish to slate. Seed capsules are green when young, but as they mature and ripen, they change to a yellowish brown. The opium poppy usually grows to a height of two to four feet. The drug opium is obtained from the milky latex exuded from the cut surfaces of unripe seed capsules.

Pharmacology

Morphine, probably the most effective painkiller known to medicine, acts largely on the sensory nerve cells of the brain, blocking messages of pain from other parts of the body. Morphine is also a stimulant, inducing euphoria and dispelling anxieties.

Heroin, a further refinement of morphine, is so dangerous that its use is forbidden in medicine.

Codeine, also derived from opium, is a prime ingredient in many cough syrups because it suppresses the cough reflex. It is also an analgesic that relieves minor pain.

Still another derivative, papaverine, is a muscle relaxant that blocks the nerve impulses responsible for muscular contractions. It is used to treat intestinal and stomach spasms as well as the respiratory spasms triggered by asthma attacks.

During the 19th and early 20th centuries, hundreds of different patent medicines that contained opiates were sold in America and abroad. Most were used to relieve aches and pains, but several (paragoric, for example) were used to control diarrhea. Opium's greatest use was by women who took it to relieve menstrual pain; in 1900, female addicts outnumbered male addicts three to one, almost the exact opposite of the situation today.

Toxicology

Opium latex contains at least 25 different alkaloids, along with many other constituents. Most of the action of opium is attributed to morphine, its preponderant component (as much as 10 percent by weight).

Other important alkaloids are codeine, thebaine, papaverine, and nar-cotine. All opiates act on the medulla, the part of the brain that controls breathing. A strong opiate dose will slow breathing, and an overdose will stop it altogether.

Symptoms

Symptoms vary with the opiate taken and its degree of toxicity. Acute intoxication will produce euphoria, flushing, itching of the skin, miosis (prolonged contraction of the pupil of the eye; pinpoint pupils), spasti-city, cyanosis, drowsiness, decreased respiratory rate and depth, hypo-tension, bradycardia, and decreased body temperature. Coma precedes death, which is usually due to respiratory failure.

Treatment

Gastric lavage should be administered immediately. If the intoxication is acute, the victim should be given naloxone intravenously. (Naloxone does not depress respiration, which could prove fatal.) Victims should be kept in the hospital for 24 hours after recovery because the effects of naloxone wear off rapidly, and respiratory depression may recur within hours.

PEYOTE

HOW IT GETS PEOPLE

Species: Lophophora williamsii

HABITAT

CLIMATIC ZONE

CLIMATIC ZONE

RATING

Europeans learned about peyote in the 16th century, when the Spanish first arrived in the New World, where the drug had been in use for hundreds of years. One early Spanish chronicler, writing of the Aztec and Chichimeca Indians' use of peyote, said it was helpful in "sustaining them and giving them the courage to fight and not feel fear, nor hunger, nor thirst; and they say it protects them from danger."

Assuming that anything that altered people's mental states (what is now called hallucinogenic) had to be the devil's tool, the conquering

Spaniards outlawed its use among the Aztecs. Peyote continued to be an important part of the Indians' religious lives, but from then on, they kept their practices quiet. As a result, much of the Indian ritual connected with peyote remained unknown to non-Indians until the mid–20th century. The use of peyote as a religious sacrament is called peyotism.

Peyote is a member of the cactus family. To prepare it for consumption, a harvester cuts off the "button," or tip, then sun–dries it. The result is a brown, discoidal (shaped like a disk) "mescal button" that can last for long periods of time and that is eaten or ground up to make a tea.

The Tarahumara Indians believed that when Father Sun left the earth to dwell above, he left peyote behind to cure humanity's ills and woes; they claim the peyote sings and talks when it grows and that, when gathered, it will continue to sing in the gatherer's bag, this being how God speaks to them. The Indians' annual peyote–collecting pilgrimage is highly religious; pilgrims are forbidden many adult experiences, such as sex, during this reenactment of the original peyote quest by their ancestors.

Peyotism began to spread northward from Mexico in the 18th century. It entered south Texas (where the plant commonly grows),

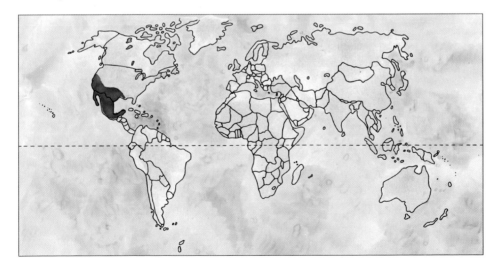

probably via the Apaches and Kiowas, who took the Mexican peyote ceremony and remodeled it into a "vision-quest" ritual, typical among the Plains Indians. From them it slowly spread to the neighboring Comanches, Wichitas, Otos, and Delawares, and then to numerous other tribes. Frederick J. Dockstader, author of *Great North American Indians*, believes that the reason for this rapid dispersal was yet another European quest for land, which resulted in many native inhabitants being forced off their land and becoming nomadic.

The upheaval deprived the Indians of much of their social identity, personal freedom, dignity, and, most of all, their rights and spiritual beliefs. Many turned to peyotism, a messianic faith that taught the worship of one God, emphasized self-reliance, sought to overcome social disintegration by collective ritual (using peyote), forbade the use of alcohol, and gathered strength through trying to unite the scattered tribes.

In 1916 the Native American Church was officially established in Oklahoma with 12,000 members. For decades, the use of peyote was opposed by many mainstream church groups, and by the U.S. Food and Drug Administration (which banned it in 1938). However, a 1970 court ruling exempted its use as a religious sacrament, and it is still used today by the 250,000 members of the Native American Church.

During the 1960s, when the use of hallucinogenic or psychedelic drugs began to spread, many young people took peyote in order to experience what is said to be a kaleidoscopic display of indescribably rich, colored visions and changes of perception in hearing, feeling, and taste. These visions usually start about three hours after ingestion and begin with flashes and scintillations in color, often followed by a sequence of incredible shapes, from simple geometric figures to unfamiliar and grotesque objects. But many users, especially first-time users, took too many (6 to 12 buttons are normally consumed) and became seriously ill. And although most of the symptoms eventually fade away, even without medical care, there can be serious, long-range psychotic reactions requiring long-term therapy.

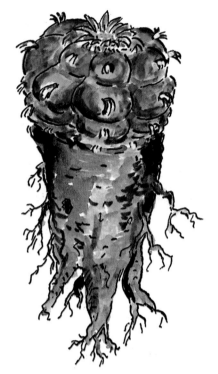

**Peyote is reportedly the most powerful
hallucinogenic plant in existence.**

Name/Description

The word *peyote* is a Spanish deviation from an Indian word for caterpil-
lar and refers to this cactus's downy covering. The two species of peyote
are *Lophophora williamsii*, found in southern Texas and northern Mexico,
and *L. diffusa*, native to central Mexico. These low-growing, spineless
cacti resemble small, puffy cushions and are about two inches tall,
growing out of a large, branched, perennial rootstock about three inches

in diameter. The bluish green (yellowish green in *L. diffusa*) fleshy body has several tubercles (protuberances) separated by hollow ribs. Brushlike hairs extend from its areoles (the minute meshes on the surface of the plant), and there are pale pink or white flowers (yellow or white in *L. diffusa*) resembling daisies in the center of the plant. The fruit is a pink berry; when ripe, the seeds are black. The taste is very bitter and disagreeable.

Pharmacology

Peyote serves a religious purpose for some, but it has no known medicinal application.

Toxicology

Peyote's "buttons," or crowns, contain 30 active constituents, the most important being two types of alkaloids: phenylethylamines and iso-quinolines. The action of the alkaloids is somewhat similar to, although less potent than, the highly publicized LSD (lysergic acid diethylamide). The white crystalline alkaloid mescaline is responsible for the visual hallucinations.

Symptoms

Symptoms vary greatly, depending on the number of buttons ingested and the state of physical and psychological health of the person taking them. Following intoxication by ingestion of fresh or dried buttons, there will be a combination of some of the following symptoms: nausea, thirst, euphoria, ataxia (irregularity of muscular action), tremor, headache, pupil dilation, blurred vision, dizziness, circulatory depression, and loss of sense of time, often accompanied by severe stomach pain with vomiting and diarrhea.

Treatment

If the victim has not vomited, give syrup of ipecac to induce vomiting. Keep reassuring the victim that most of the symptoms will disappear in a few hours. Many intoxicated victims have severe psychotic reactions requiring professional medical care.

POINSETTIA

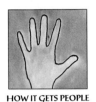

HOW IT GETS PEOPLE

Species: Euphorbia pulcherrima

HOW IT GETS PEOPLE

HABITAT

HABITAT

HABITAT

CLIMATIC ZONE

CLIMATIC ZONE

RATING

To many people, Christmas comes in red and green: the beautiful evergreen Christmas tree, the holly and mistletoe, the brilliant scarlet poinsettia. In that festive season, careful parents consider the safety of their children; they worry about youngsters getting a mild shock from electric Christmas tree lights, for example. But most think little about placing an attractive, tempting—and toxic—poinsettia within the easy reach of little hands. Eating just one leaf of this plant can make a child extremely ill; in a few rare cases, children have died after ingesting poinsettia leaves.

Some years ago, a tragic news story told of an army officer at Fort Shafter, Hawaii, whose two-year-old son ate a few poinsettia leaves and died after first suffering vomiting, diarrhea, and delirium. Usually, the poinsettia leaves' bitter, acrid taste stops children from sucking on them before they seriously poison themselves, but sometimes it does not stop them soon enough.

Native to tropical Mexico and Central America, where it is called *Noche Buena* (Good Night) in reference to Christmas Eve, poinsettia was named after Joel R. Poinsett, a U.S. diplomat who introduced it to the United States. There, it was quickly adopted as a symbol of Christmas. The poinsettia, also known as Christmas flower and Christmas star, now appears on gift paper, Christmas cards, tree decorations, and, in its most hazardous form, as centerpieces in Christmas punchbowls: some hosts have frozen clusters of the plant's bright red leaves into ice cubes as a festive decoration. Sooner or later, of course, the ice melts, the punch becomes contaminated, and unsuspecting guests fall sick.

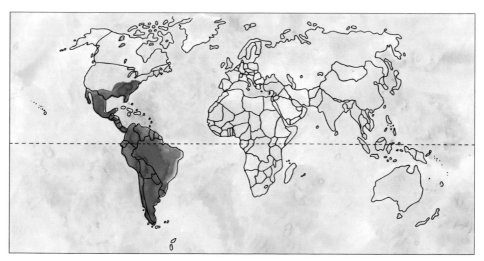

Name/Description

Poinsettia is a showy shrub with drooping, wandlike branches bearing dark green leaves from three to six inches in length. Because the top leaves are red, pink, or cream colored, they are believed by most people to be the flowers, which are actually tiny yellow blossoms surrounded by the colored leaves. Growing from 2 to 10 feet tall, poinsettias contain an irritant milky sap, which can disturb the sensitive tissues of the digestive system.

Pharmacology

Mexican herbalists boil the leaves in water to obtain a white, crystalline sugar that is used to dress wounds. The plant is otherwise of no medical interest.

Toxicology

The toxic principles of the sap are a complex of substances including alkaloids, glycosides, and others. Euphorbon, found therein, is highly caustic.

Symptoms

Entering the eye, poinsettia sap produces irritation, conjunctivitis (in-flammation of the mucous membrane on the eyelid's inner surface), and in extreme cases, blindness. Swallowing any part of the leaves usually results in immediate nausea and vomiting, occasionally followed by abdominal pain, gastritis (inflammation of the stomach and lining), diarrhea, delirium, and—very rarely—death.

Treatment

For eye irritation, wash out the eye with clear water, and see an eye doctor if the problem persists. For ingestion, if the victim has not vomited, give syrup of ipecac to induce vomiting; a doctor may order gastric lavage instead. Because protracted vomiting after ingestion can lead to dehydration, the patient should be given copious fluids.

Though popularly used as a Christmas
decoration, poinsettias can prove fatal to
children who nibble on their leaves.

POKEWEED

HOW IT GETS PEOPLE

Species: Phytolacca americana
and P. decandra

CLIMATIC ZONE

HABITAT

HABITAT

HABITAT

RATING

Eat your greens! This admonition could prove dangerous in the south-eastern United States, where cooked pokeweed is a popular dish: when served raw or inadequately prepared, pokeweed can cause violent illness, even—in very rare cases—death.

Pokeweed's young leaves, also known as poke salad, are delicious, according to many southerners, especially when seasoned with bacon drippings and pepper. But preparation is crucial. The plant should be harvested only in the spring, when its leaves and shoots are tender; as it matures, pokeweed becomes increasingly indigestible. Those planning to cook stems as well as leaves should do so only before the stems change from green to pink in color, and should be extremely careful to avoid any part of the root. The greens should be blanched (covered with boiling water), drained, then gently boiled and drained again. All the cooking water (sometimes called pot liquor) should be discarded. Some cooks serve the pokeweed at this point; others prefer to fry the boiled greens in bacon fat or butter first.

Pokeweed roots have sometimes been mistaken for parsnips or horseradish—an error that can lead to serious problems, as the roots are toxic at all times, especially for young children. Even people who never touch a vegetable can experience gastric distress from pokeweed—if they eat game that has fed on pokeweed berries. Children, too, are often attracted to the clusters of dark purple fruits (sometimes called ink-berries); their juice is reportedly quite flavorful, but it contains toxic tannin. Medical literature contains numerous sad stories connected with children and pokeberries: one two-year-old Rhode Island girl feasted on several handfuls, went into a coma three days later, and died

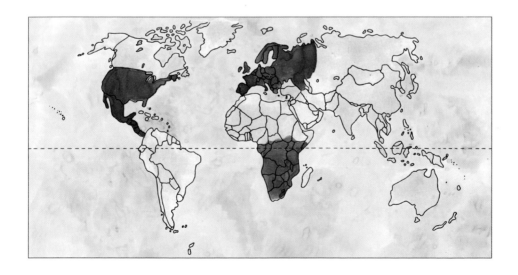

in two weeks. Another youngster, this one five years old, died after eating crushed pokeberries, which she had turned into "grape juice" by crushing and adding water.

Name/Description

Pokeweed, also known as pokeberry, inkberry, or scoke, is a coarse, strong–smelling, perennial shrub. Its thick red stems bear long green leaves, which measure 4 to 12 inches at maturity, and greenish white to purplish flowers, which give way to berries in the late summer. The berries are oblate (flattened at the ends) and greenish white, later turning purplish black. The plant's poisonous root is thick, often measuring as much as six inches in diameter. The whole plant reaches heights of up to 12 feet.

Pharmacology

Once a widely used medicine, pokeweed has fallen out of favor with the medical community. North American settlers used to make extracts of pokeweed roots and berries, taking them to cure everything from skin diseases and conjunctivitis to chronic rheumatism and indigestion. Our forebears also applied the berry juice to cancerous skin ulcers.

Toxicology

Pokeberry roots and leaves, which contain triterpenoid saponins and the toxic alkaloids phytolaccin and phytolaccagenin, are poisonous. Except for the berries, the plant becomes more toxic as it matures.

Symptoms

Pokeweed poisoning usually takes effect about two hours after the plant is eaten. It produces a bitter taste and a burning sensation from the mouth to the stomach, violent vomiting that can be of long duration, retching, abdominal cramps, diarrhea, blurred vision, drowsiness, and sweating. These symptoms may continue for 48 hours.

**Many unwitting children suffer pokeweed poisoning
by using the plant to color food and drinks.**

Treatment

Induce vomiting or administer gastric lavage. Analgesics may be given
for pain, with replacement fluids being given frequently to prevent
dehydration (especially necessary for children). Otherwise, treat symp–
tomatically. If one lives, recovery is usually within 48 hours.

RHODODENDRON

HOW IT GETS PEOPLE

Family: Ericaceae, comprising
about 800 species of the genus
Rhododendron

HOW IT GETS PEOPLE

HABITAT

HABITAT

HABITAT

CLIMATIC ZONE

CLIMATIC ZONE

CLIMATIC ZONE

RATING

Throughout history, the rhododendron has been both friend and foe
to humanity, both medicine and poison. Its graceful, elegant flowers
offer pleasure to the eye, and its leaves have been used to treat everything from rheumatism to bronchitis to high blood pressure. It is also
the source of one of the deadliest poisons in all nature. As botanist

David G. Leach has put it, "The rhododendron, a dramatically beautiful springtime flower without evil reputation, is the plant with the most lurid past of all."

In a magazine article entitled "The Ancient Curse of the Rhododendron," Leach goes on to relate several astonishing tales about the lovely but dangerous shrub. One of them involves Xenophon, a historian and military leader of ancient Greece whose responsibility, in 401 B.C., was to guide 10,000 Greek soldiers back to Greece from deep inside Asia Minor. After many miles of hard marching, the army was approaching its goal when it stopped to rest on the Black Sea coast of Turkey, an area dotted with beehives—and vast banks of rhododendrons.

The hungry soldiers happily gorged themselves with honey from the hives, but soon afterward, reported the horrified Xenophon, they "lost their senses, and were seized with vomiting and purging, none of them being able to stand on their legs. Those who ate but a little were like men very drunk, and those who ate much, like madmen, and some like dying persons." The men finally recovered and proceeded home, but they probably never forgot the botanical lesson they had learned at such cost:

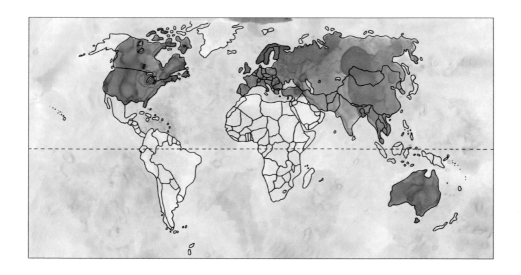

that rhododendron nectar is poisonous and that bees who gather it produce poisoned honey.

Various primitive peoples also knew of—and profitably used—the poison in the rhododendron. Archaeologists have described ancient tribes whose members pounded rhododendron leaves into a pulp, threw them into pools, then gathered up the poisoned fish as they rose to the water's surface. When cleaned, the fish were apparently nontoxic. The Chinese also employed the shrub, but in a much different manner. In China, rhododendron leaves have been commonly sold in drug shops for centuries. Used in China for treating circulatory disorders, they are also rolled up and smoked for relief from asthma attacks and sometimes made into an extract for treating chronic bronchitis.

Not all medical uses, however, have been as successful as those of the Chinese. In the late 18th century, John Gmelin, a German chemistry professor working in Russia, incorrectly attributed arthritis cures to a "tea" prepared from dried Siberian rhododendron leaves. After reading Gmelin's reports, another German physician, Alexander Koelpin, began to treat arthritis sufferers with the tea. Despite mixed results—several of his patients died, and most experienced severe breathing and blood–pressure problems—Koelpin decided the rhododendron mixture did indeed relieve arthritis pain, and in 1779, he published a treatise on the subject, *Practical Observations About the Use of the Siberian Snow Rose*.

Koelpin's book impressed the European medical community, and soon doctors from Scotland to Russia were subjecting their own patients to the tea regimen. No one will ever know how many thousands of tormented arthritics were dosed with the dangerous tea, but it remained, astonishingly, in steady use for more than a century after publication of Koelpin's *Practical Observations*.

No longer medically prescribed, rhododendron is now cultivated primarily for its handsome appearance. It still poses a threat, however: in some parts of Asia, farmers regularly muzzle their cattle to prevent them from grazing on rhododendron. And in England, where the plant graces many parks and estates, the owners of ponies and horses have

Whereas mild rhododendron intoxication resembles drunkenness, acute poisoning produces a behavior more like madness.

learned—often too late—that their animals must be watched carefully, lest they sample the toxic leaves of the deadly "rhodie."

Name/Description

Rhododendron, which grows wild and in cultivation around the world, has leathery, alternate, long, ovate, and glassy evergreen leaves. The plant's showy flowers usually range in color from white to red, but the majority are pink with spots of coloration in the upper part of the throat. Some recently developed hybrids produce purple, yellow, or orange blossoms. Growing to heights of up to 40 feet (although the *Rhododendron giganteum* of Yunnan grows to 80 feet), the plants thrive in well–drained, often acidic soil, particularly in woodlands. Sizes and shapes vary with the species.

Pharmacology

Rhododendron leaves and their extracts have figured prominently in the pharmacology of many nations, but modern medical science has few uses for it. A possible exception is work in progress during the early 1990s in Germany; there, pharmaceutical manufacturers are experimenting with a new rhododendron extract for the treatment of high blood pressure.

Toxicology

The rhododendron's leaves are toxic, as is honey produced from the nectar of its flowers. The main toxic principles are andromedotoxins (considered resinoids), which cause a narcotic action on the higher centers of the brain and also reduce blood pressure.

Symptoms

Ingestion produces an immediate but temporary burning sensation in the mouth; it is followed several hours later by excess salivation, vomiting, diarrhea, and a prickling sensation in the skin. Headache, muscular weakness, and visual disturbances may also be present. Acute poisonings produce convulsions, coma, and death.

Treatment

With most mild poisonings, the victim recovers within 24 hours. If a patient vomits copiously, he or she may need fluid replacement. In more acute cases, a doctor may call for respiratory support, and, if the victim's heart rate is weak, administer atropine.

ROSARY PEA

HOW IT GETS PEOPLE

Species: Abrus precatorius

HOW IT GETS PEOPLE

HABITAT

HABITAT

HABITAT

HABITAT

CLIMATIC ZONE

RATING

Rosary peas are actually the colorful seeds of a tropical vine indigenous to India. Known there since ancient times as *rati*, the seeds were used to weigh gold, each rati weighing about one carat. The rati was used to measure the famed, 106–carat Kohinoor diamond of India, now part of the British crown jewels. The root of this leguminous plant, a member of the pea family, is called *gunga* in India, where it was used medicinally as a demulcent (a soothing ointment). Gunga was also notorious as a poison, employed both on livestock and, not infrequently, on human beings.

In the New World, the plant's seeds, also known as "prayer beads," have long been used to make rosaries, although this practice is now increasingly discouraged or outlawed. Other products made from the seeds include necklaces, rattles, bracelets, and good luck charms (hence another name for them: "lucky bean").

The mature seed of the rosary pea is not toxic unless its hard coating is broken. It can even be swallowed whole without causing harm. But just one cracked or split seed, if ingested, can prove fatal, even with immediate and intensive medical care. The seed's poisons are just as dangerous if they enter the body through a cut: deaths have occurred when workers stringing the colorful seeds have pricked their fingers. Numerous children, too, have been poisoned by these tempting but lethal playthings.

In the past, the rosary pea's highly toxic seeds were frequently carried back to Britain, Europe, and the United States by tourists returning from Caribbean and other tropical resort areas. Recognizing its dangers, most countries now prohibit its use in consumer products; some have even made its cultivation illegal.

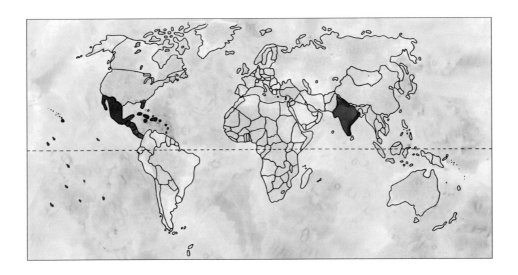

Name/Description

A slender, tropical, twining vine, the rosary pea has a woody base and winds around other plants, fences, or on the ground, growing up to 20 feet in length. Its compound leaves are light sensitive and droop at night and on cloudy days; its inconspicuous flowers are reddish purple or white. The fruit, a legume, is an ovate pod about one and a half inches long. As it dries, the pod splits open to reveal three to five hard-coated, scarlet, pea-sized seeds, each bearing a small black spot at the point of its attachment to the pod.

Pharmacology

European doctors once treated certain eye diseases with an infusion and paste made from rosary pea seeds, but the plant is no longer considered medicinally useful.

Toxicology

The seeds of the rosary pea contain abrin, a phytotoxin and one of the deadliest poisons known. Abrin inhibits protein synthesis in growing intestinal-wall cells and damages blood cells.

Symptoms

Symptoms of poisoning by touch and ingestion are the same. Onset of the symptoms may be delayed several hours, or even up to three days, depending on the number of seeds ingested and their degree of pulverization or on the amount of poison that entered the body through a cut or sore. Both means of poisoning produce nausea, vomiting, acute gastroenteritis (inflammation of the lining of the stomach and intestines), chills, weak but fast pulse, circulatory collapse, convulsions, and, occasionally, death.

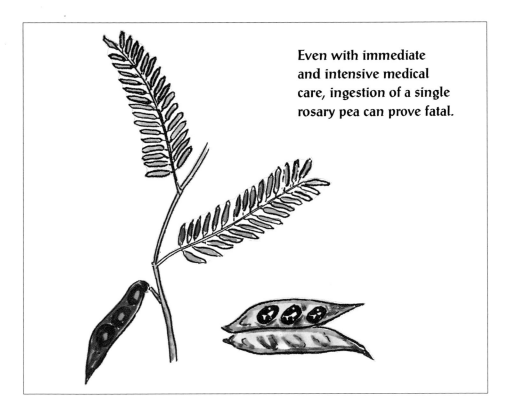

Even with immediate and intensive medical care, ingestion of a single rosary pea can prove fatal.

Treatment

Give syrup of ipecac to induce vomiting. A physician may order gastric lavage and prescribe diazepam to control convulsions. Even with the best medical care, the fatality rate is extremely high: about 1 in 20 people who have contracted abrin poisoning will die.

SNOW-ON-THE-MOUNTAIN

HOW IT GETS PEOPLE

Species: Euphorbia marginata

HOW IT GETS PEOPLE

HABITAT

HABITAT

CLIMATIC ZONE

RATING

Snow-on-the-mountain sounds crisp, cool, and fresh, but this member of the spurge (Euphorbiaceae) family can burn skin, remove hair, brand cattle, poison arrows, and, if taken internally, poison humans. The plant's family name should serve as a warning: *spurge* comes from an old French word meaning "purge," which is one of the effects of this plant's sap on the digestive system. Hundreds of years ago, a botanist described snow-on-the-mountain as "a strong cathartic [a purgative or laxative] working violently by vomit and stool, but is very offensive to the stomach and bowels by reason of its sharp corrosive quality."

The plant's milky sap, released when a stem is cut or broken, has earned spurges another name in England: "Virgin Mary's nipple." Far from being pure or nourishing, however, the sap is toxic: it has been used to remove warts as well as to poison arrows and remove hair. As one early writer noted, spurges "abound with a hot and acrid juice which, when applied outwardly, eats away warts and other excrescences."

Farmers have reported on horses whose forelegs have been blistered and stripped of hair while they were working in grain fields where spurge also grew. In Texas, ranchers have used the highly caustic sap of spurges, in place of the traditional red–hot iron, to brand their cattle.

Bees that feed on the nectar of snow–on–the–mountain produce poisonous honey. Some health authorities fear an increase in this toxic sweet: more and more gardeners are cultivating snow–on–the–moun-tain, a handsome plant that thrives in almost any temperate climate, in their border groupings and rock gardens.

Name/Description

Snow-on-the-mountain is a bushy annual plant that usually reaches a height of some two feet. It has ovate leaves, one to three inches in length; the uppermost leaves are prominently banded in white, which, at a distance, makes them look like white flowers. The plant bears clusters of small white blossoms and roundish, three-lobed capsules. Popular as an ornamental, snow-on-the-mountain contains a whitish sap, or latex, as do all members of the spurge family.

Pharmacology

Some spurges have medicinal value; the emetic ipecac, for example, comes from the *E. ipecacuanhae*, or ipecac spurge. Early herbalists pre-scribed snow-on-the-mountain as a depilatory and wart remover, but the plant has no current pharmaceutical application.

Toxicology

The toxic principles of snow-on-the-mountain are a complex of sub-stances including alkaloids and glycosides. The plant contains the caustic substance euphorbon.

Symptoms

Taken internally, snow-on-the-mountain sap produces painful inflam-mation of the mouth and throat, severe gastroenteritis (inflammation of the membrane lining the stomach and intestines), nausea, vomiting, and diarrhea. Ingestion also occasionally causes dilation of the pupils, giddi-ness, delirium, and, in acute poisonings, convulsions.

External contact with the sap produces reddening and swelling of the skin in two to eight hours. This inflammation can increase in intensity during the following 12 hours, forming blisters and pustules. The reac-tions can be painful, especially if the skin is cut, but they generally disappear in a few days, leaving no scars. Latex in the eyes can result in

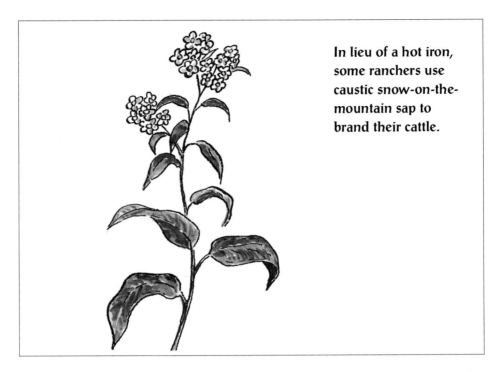

In lieu of a hot iron, some ranchers use caustic snow-on-the-mountain sap to brand their cattle.

severe conjunctivitis (inflammation of the mucous membrane lining the inner surface of the eyelids) and choroiditis (inflammation of the dark, vascular membrane of the eye).

Treatment

If the sap has been ingested and the patient has not vomited, give syrup of ipecac to induce vomiting; a doctor may choose to administer gastric lavage instead. After vomiting, the patient should drink copious fluids. To relieve itching resulting from contact, apply a soothing lotion such as calamine and an anesthetic cream containing benzocaine. Antihis–tamines may be given, as well as antibiotics for secondary infections. Conjunctivitis and choroiditis of the eye usually heal completely after several weeks of medical attention.

APPENDIX I:
Poisons and Toxins

A *poison* is defined as a substance that through its chemical action usually kills, injures, or impairs an organism it has entered or come into contact with. The human organism is vulnerable to a wide variety of poisons in the environment. Synthetic poisons are seemingly everywhere; they can be found in household products such as disinfectants, cleaners, hair sprays, cosmetics, paints, and glues; in fumes, gases, and vapors from industrial waste products; and in lawn fertilizers and insect sprays. Most of these synthetic poisons are industrial in origin and are thus relatively new. But *biotoxins*, or naturally produced poisons, were here even before the human race entered the picture.

There are four primary types of biotoxin. Microbial toxins are produced by microscopic organisms, such as bacteria and algae. Zootoxins are the venoms produced by poisonous animals and insects, such as rattlesnakes and hornets. Mushrooms and other fungi produce biotoxins known as mycotoxins. Plant biotoxins are called phytotoxins. (Some plants contain toxins only in certain parts, such as the roots or leaves. The plants discussed in this volume are toxic throughout, although the toxin may be more highly concentrated in one part of the plant.) It is thought that biotoxins act primarily as defensive or protective agents, helping plant species to survive and prosper.

Mycotoxins and phytotoxins can be just as dangerous as synthetic poisons or animal venoms. They can also be extremely helpful. A large dose of a certain mycotoxin or phytotoxin might have a deadly effect on the human heart, whereas a smaller dose of the same substance might prove to be beneficial to a diseased heart. People have been aware of these properties and have been using these substances to kill or to cure one another since the dawn of civilization, and thus the study and classification of plant poisons is an age-old discipline.

In the 1st century A.D., the Greek physician Dioscorides wrote *De materia medica*, the first encyclopedic work on medicinal botany. In the early 11th century, the Persian physician and philosopher Avicenna compiled his *Canon of Medicine*, which for centuries remained the standard reference volume on biotoxins and their antidotes. In the meantime, various practitioners of traditional or folk medicine from cultures around the world continued to collect and pass on information regarding botanical poisons and cures; much of this data was eventually incorporated into the mainstream of medical research and practice. During the 19th and 20th centuries, a vast wealth of new information concerning plant poisons and their effects—both positive and negative—has been gathered and put to use, although our knowledge and understanding of the subject is by no means complete. Indeed, many modern botanists feel that the curative potential of plants has only just begun to be realized. It is conceivable that somewhere deep in the South American jungles or in some shadowy forest of the Pacific Northwest, an unlovely mushroom or a blossoming flower holds the secret to curing cancer or one of the other ailments that currently plague humankind.

APPENDIX II:
Shock

A term that many people use informally, *shock*, in medical terms, is a profoundly disturbing, often fatal condition characterized by a failure of the circulatory system to maintain an adequate blood supply to vital organs. It can be caused by severe injury, blood loss, or disease.

Shock is a state in which perfusion (passage of blood to the vessels) and the blood flow to peripheral tissues are inadequate to sustain life because of insufficient levels of carbon dioxide in the blood or maldistribution of blood flow. Shock is associated with diminished peripheral circulation, hypotension (abnormally low blood pressure), and oliguria (diminished urine output).

Other symptoms are lethargy, confusion, and somnolence (unnatural drowsiness). The victim's hands and feet are cold, moist, and often cyanotic (having a bluish discoloration as a result of insufficient oxygen in the blood), and his or her pulse is weak and rapid.

Untreated, shock is usually fatal. Treatment depends on the cause, the presence of a preexisting or complicating illness, and the time between onset and diagnosis. The victim should be kept warm, with legs raised slightly to improve circulation. The victim's airway and ventilation should be checked, and respiratory assistance should be given if necessary. The head of a shock victim should be turned to one side to prevent choking on his or her own vomit.

FURTHER READING

Creekmore, Hubert. *Daffodils Are Dangerous*. New York: Walker and Co., 1966.

Emboden, William A. *Bizarre Plants, Magical, Monstrous, Mythical*. New York: Macmillan, 1974.

Graf, Alfred Byrd. *Exotica: Pictorial Cyclopedia of Exotic Plants from Tropical and Near Tropical Regions*. East Rutherford, NJ: Roehrs Co., 1976.

Hardin, James W., and Jay M. Arena. *Human Poisoning from Native and Cultivated Plants*. Durham, NC: Duke University Press, 1974.

Kingsbury, John M. *Poisonous Plants of the U.S. and Canada*. Englewood Cliffs, NJ: Prentice Hall, 1964.

Lampe, Dr. Kenneth F., and Mary Ann McCann. *AMA Handbook of Poisonous and Injurious Plants*. Chicago: American Medical Association, 1985.

Richardson, Joan. *Wild Edible Plants of New England, Including Poisonous Plants Often Encountered: A Field Guide*. Chester, CT: Globe Pequot Press, 1981.

INDEX

Missy Allen is a writer and photographer whose work has appeared in *Time*, *Geo*, *Vogue*, *Paris-Match*, *Elle*, and many European publications. Allen holds a master's degree in education from Boston University. Before her marriage to Michel Peissel, she worked for the Harvard School of Public Health and was director of admissions at Harvard's Graduate School of Arts and Sciences.

Michel Peissel is an anthropologist, explorer, inventor, and author. He has studied at the Harvard School of Business, Oxford University, and the Sorbonne. Called "the last true adventurer of the 20th century," Peissel discovered 14 Mayan sites in the eastern Yucatán at the age of 21 and was the youngest member ever elected to the New York Explorers Club. He is also one of the world's foremost experts on the Himalayas, where he has led 14 major expeditions. Peissel has written 14 books, which have been published in 83 editions in 15 countries.

When not found in their fisherman's house in Cadaqués, Spain, with their two young children, Peissel and Allen can be found trekking across the Himalayas or traveling in Central America.

ACKNOWLEDGMENTS

The authors would like to thank Lisa Bateman for her editorial assistance; Brian Rankin for his careful typing; Carla Maristany for her graphic designs; and Linnie Greason, Heather Moulton, and Luis Abiega for so kindly allowing their lives to be infiltrated by these creepy crawlies and ferocious fauna.

CREDITS

All the original watercolor illustrations are by Michel Peissel. The geo-graphic distribution maps are by Diana Blume.